A half-mile up, suspended by nylon wings and the promise of good lift, life hangs on a pledge. Richard Bach made that pledge, fifty years before, to return to the frightened child he used to be and teach him everything he had learned from living. His promise went unfulfilled until one day, hovering between earth and sky, Richard encounters Dickie Bach, age nine—irrepressible challenger of every notion Richard embraces. . . .

In this exhilarating adventure, Richard and Dickie probe the timeless questions both need answered if either is to be whole: Why does growing spiritually mean never growing up? Can we peacefully coexist with the consequences of our choices? Why is it that only by running from safety can we make our wildest dreams take flight?

RUNNING FROM SAFETY

Books by Richard Bach

STRANGER TO THE GROUND

BIPLANE

NOTHING BY CHANCE

JONATHAN LIVINGSTON SEAGULL

A GIFT OF WINGS

ILLUSIONS: THE ADVENTURES OF A RELUCTANT MESSIAH

THERE'S NO SUCH PLACE AS FAR AWAY

THE BRIDGE ACROSS FOREVER: A LOVESTORY

ONE

Running from Safety

An Adventure of the Spirit

Delta

Published by
Delta Publishing
a division of
Bantam Doubleday Dell Publishing Group, Inc.
1540 Broadway
New York, New York 10036

This book is autobiographical. However, some names and other identifying details have been changed to protect the privacy of the individuals involved.

WARNING!
The principles in this book were developed in risk-filled environments by an unlicensed amateur. They are not complete, nor have their implications been fully tested.

DO NOT TRY THESE IDEAS AT HOME!
The author is neither liable nor responsible for personal or family catastrophes which will likely occur as a result of the reader's casual decision to apply similar choices in daily life.

ISBN: 0-385-31528-7

Reprinted by arrangement with William Morrow and Company, Inc.

Printed in the United States of America
Published simultaneously in Canada

December 1995

10 9 8 7 6 5 4 3 2 1

BVG

Introduction

My truth has been a long time refining. I've explored and drilled for it with hope and intuition, filtered and condensed it the best I could with reflection, then run it through my engines, wary at first, to see what would happen.

There have been a few backfires, all right, an explosion or two on the racetrack when I learned how volatile any home-mixed philosophy must be. Sooty but wiser, I blinked a while ago to realize I've been running my mind on this peculiar fuel much of my life. Even today, cautiously reckless, drop by drop, I'm gradually raising the octane.

I didn't choose to brew my own facts for the fun of it, however, or because I never filled up on regular. Passionate to discover reasons to be and themes to live by, I surveyed religions as a teenager, studied Aristotle and Descartes and

Kant in night-school colleges while I was yet a line pilot in the Air Force.

Last course finished, steps heavy and slow on the sidewalk, I was gripped in strange depression. As best I could understand from classrooms, these gentlemen knew less about who we are and why we're here than I did, and I barely had a glimmer.

Heavy intellects, they were, cruising stratospheres above the ceiling of my government fighter planes. I was willing to borrow shamelessly from their insight to build my own, yet it was all I could do, listening in class, to keep from screaming, *"Who cares?"*

Practical Socrates I admired for his choice to die for principle when escape would have been easy. Others were not so compelling. All those tight-packed pages, microscopic letters, and at last their wise conclusion: You're on your own, Richard. How can we know what works for you?

Studies finished, I walked aimless down the night, footsteps echoing to an empty campus, no place in mind to go.

I took this course for guidance, I thought, I needed a compass to take me through jungles. Organized religions for me were teetery bridges, weak-tied twigs that snapped at the first pressure, a child's question turning impossible mystery. Why do religions cling to Unanswerable Questions? Don't they know *That's unanswerable* is no answer?

Over and again I'd meet a new theology, and every time would come the test: Do I take this belief to become my life?

Each time I asked, tried my weight on it, the spider-stick jackstraws trembled and creaked, then all at once collapsed in front of me, steps tearing off, tumbling down out of sight.

I'd grab the world, cringe back from the edge thankful not to have been killed in the fall. How would it feel, to give one's heart to a religion that guarantees the planet will dissolve in fire come December 31, then wake up New Year's Day to songs of snowbirds? Sheepish, is how it would feel.

From behind me as I walked, a woman's footsteps in the night. I angled right, to let her pass.

Now I've finished my course in twenty philosophies, I thought, history's brightest stars, and every one has failed. All I asked was that they show me a way of thinking about the universe to guide me in daily life—not too hard a task for Thomas Aquinas or Georg Wilhelm Friedrich Hegel, you'd think. Their answers worked for them, but their daily life was on a different moon from mine.

"Was your study for nothing?" she said. "They've just taught you what you've been hoping to find all these years, and you don't even know it?"

A flash of vexation . . . the woman wasn't passing me by, she was listening to my mind!

"Excuse me?" I said, cold as could be.

Dark hair with a bold streak of blond, twenty years older than I, plain, not so well dressed, unaware of what I do to people who demolish my quiet-times.

"They gave you what you came to learn!" she said. "Your life is turning tonight, can't you feel it?"

I looked back along the sidewalk, no one else in sight. She's got the wrong person, I knew. She wasn't from philosophy class, she was no one I had ever seen before.

"I don't believe we've met," I told her.

Instead of freezing, she laughed. " 'I don't believe we've met.' " She waved her hand in front of my eyes. "They've taught you they don't have answers! Don't you get it? Nobody has answers for you except one!"

Heaven help, I thought. She's going to tell me Jesus Christ is my Redeemer and she's going to wash me in the blood of the Lamb. Must I hurl Bible quotes to drive her off?

I sighed. "When Jesus said *No one comes to the Father but by me* he did not mean me the ex-journeyman carpenter but me the quest to know spirit in . . ."

"Richard!" she said. "Please!"

I stopped and faced her, waiting. Her smile was undiminished, her eyes sparkled starlight. She's a lot more pretty than plain, I thought, why didn't I notice? Does my annoyance turn others drab?

As I watched, the streetlights must have changed . . . she was not just pretty, she was beautiful.

She waited, then, till she had my complete attention. Was she changing, I wondered, and not the light? What was going on?

"Jesus doesn't have the truth you're looking for," she said. "Neither does Lao-tzu or Henry James. What you'd discover tonight, if you'd open your eyes to more than a pretty face, is . . . what?"

She waited.

"I know you, don't I?" I said.

For the first time that night she frowned.

"You're goddamn right you do!"

✦

It's been that way for as long as I can remember. Somebody's ever following me, crashing into me when I swing around corners, showing up in subways or airplane cockpits to tell me what the lesson's been for every strange event.

At first I thought these folks were phantoms, constructs of my own imagination, and at first they were. What a surprise, when the next several of these teaching souls turned out to be mortals as firmly three-dimensional as I, as startled to find me in the middle of their adventures as I was to find them in mine.

After a while I couldn't tell whether the person at watch over me and my lessons was mortal or not, and nowadays I assume they're people until they disappear in the middle of a sentence or whisk me off to alternate worlds to illustrate some fine point of metaphysics.

In the end, of course, it doesn't matter who they are. Some folks are angels without so much as the courtesy of introduction. Others I've known for years before I've seen their feathers, others still I've thought were living gospel till the minute I found they were bad news.

This book is the story of one of these encounters in my little refinery of thought, what I learned from it and how the learning changed my life.

Do my lessons match yours? Am I a fire-singed fellow angel from a racetrack you're driving too, or am I one more odd stranger muttering in the street? Some answers I'll never know.

But hurry now, or we'll be late for Chapter One.

One

I stood at the peak of the mountain, watching the wind. Way off near the horizon it gently streaked the lake, easing in my direction. It tilted a few columns of chimney-smoke in the town, two thousand feet below, stirred emerald leaves in the trees of the foothills. Delicate yarn wind-streamers on the edge of the cliff fluttered in cycles with the passing thermals, two minutes lazy, half a minute brisk.

Better some wind when I jump off the cliff, I decided, better wait for the gust.

"Are you the dummy today, or is it me?"

I turned and smiled at Ceejay Sturtevant, a flyer no taller than my shoulder, strapped into her paraglider harness, laced into helmet and boots, frazzled mascot teddy-bear

1

peering over the edge of her flight-suit pocket, her wing a pool of nylon colors laid carefully on the ground behind.

"I'm waiting for a little more wind," I told her. "You go ahead if you want."

"Thank you, Richard," she said. "Clear?"

I stood out of her way. "Clear."

She paused for a second, looking to the horizon, then all at once lunged toward the cliff. For a moment it was convincing suicide, she was racing to her doom on the rocks below. Next moment, though, her paraglider wing snapped from limp fabric to a whirlwind of wild canary and neon pink, a cloud of sheer fabrics leapt high over her head, a sudden grand Chinese kite come to rescue her from the folly of dying.

By the time her boots reached the precipice she was no longer running but flying, held in the air by cat's-cradle suspension lines rising from her harness to the giant wing.

Her husband watched as he strapped into his own harness. "Go for it, Ceejay!" he called. "Find us the lift!"

First one off the mountain is the wind-dummy, the rest of us watching, praying for rising air near the slopes, a day for long soaring flights. Prayers failing, it's calm air for simple glides to the valley floor, then hikes to the top again or rides with good-hearted drivers headed up the mountain road.

The bright canopy turned and began to rise. Cheers from the six of us waiting to fly. Then it sank again, gliding away. Groans. Chances were this was going to be one of those days when only the most skillful can stay in the air half an hour after launch.

I watched Ceejay fly for a while, then saw my thermal gust marching up the mountain: leaves shivering, branches shifting in its path, wind-streamers perking to lift. Time to fly.

Turning my back to the wind, I pulled sharply on the suspension lines and my wing rose from the grave of earth with the airy crackling rustle of a sailboat spinnaker thrown on the sky.

It was as if I had pulled my own cirrus cloud aloft, a silken rainbow thirty feet from wingtip to wingtip, lemon-lime streamers fluttering out behind the trailing edge. It pulsed overhead as I stood in the breeze: no feathers, no wax—the kite that would have kept Icarus from falling. Three thousand years late for him, I thought, just in time for me.

I squinted into the rainbow, checked suspension lines untangled, turned to face the wind.

Delicious life. I leaned into the harness and walked my kite to the edge of the cliff, as slow and heavy as a suited diver leaning to walk underwater. Then at last deliberately stepped into the air beyond the slope. Instead of dropping over the edge, the rainbow lifted me, and we flew at the speed of a walk out from the mountain, over the treetops.

"Go for it, Richard!" somebody shouted.

I pulled lightly on one brake toggle, turned and grinned at them across the sudden chasm of air to where they stood, five paragliders in silk and spiderweb, anxious to throw their gossamers into the wind and go where the sky would take them.

"Lots of lift," I called back.

Then my gust moved on, and the rising air faded past.

From eye-level, the flyers on the mountaintop rose above me as I sank away, hunting for thermals. Off to the north flew Ceejay, slanted in a tight spiral, barely holding altitude. Beneath me the mountainside dropped away, the abyss dropping below a frail air-boat.

Two years ago, I thought, this would have been high adrenaline, suspended solo by fifty strings over a half-mile plunge to earth. Now it was a lazy gentle dream of flight: no engine, no steel-and-glass cocoon around me, just the sigh of colors overhead drifting through the air.

4

A raven appeared briefly alongside, at the distance between fear and curiosity. Black eyes agog, head twisted astonished at the sight: a corn-planter, clutched by the rainbow!

I leaned back in the harness like a child in a high swing, watched the mountainside rise above me, gave up the search for lift. This is what I dreamed when I was a kid in the meadow with my newspaper kite. Swifter than eagles was part of the dream, but so was slower than butterflies, a soft loving friendship with the sky.

There below turned the green hayfield we used for a landing zone, and parked at the roadside were those who stopped to watch the paragliders fly. As I angled toward the grass, still a hundred feet up, I counted five cars waiting, and a sixth slowing to stop. It felt odd that anyone on the ground would look up and notice, my private time aloft turned public. Except at airshows, I've always felt invisible when I fly.

Ten minutes after stepping into the air I stepped out of it, slowed the wing to zero speed just at the grasstops, put one foot on the ground, then the other. The wing stayed overhead, protecting, until I was safely down, then as I tugged on the rear risers it transformed itself back into loose silk, collapsed into heaps of cloud and color around me.

Above, Ceejay and the others were dots in the sky,

hanging on, scratching for lift and finding it, working hard, thermal by thermal. They were more tenacious pilots than I, and the reward for their work was that they stayed in the air while I stood now on the ground.

I stretched the wing flat, then folded it ends to center, ends to center till it was a fluffy square in the hay; squashed the air out and rolled it into its backpack.

"Want a ride to the top?"

A voice from paragliding heaven, promising to save an hour and a half hiking.

"Thank you!" I turned and found a smallish fellow, gray hair, the friendly eyes of a college don, leaning arms-folded against his car, watching me.

"Quite some sport," he said. "You look like fireworks, up there."

"It's fun," I said, lifting the pack by one shoulder-strap and walking toward his car. "You don't know how much I appreciate the ride."

"I can imagine," he said, "and I'm glad to do it." He offered his hand. "My name's Shepherd."

"Richard," I said.

I set the wing in its pack on the rear seat and slid into the passenger's side of a rusting 1955 Ford. A book lay face-down next to him on the tattered upholstery of the front seat.

"Turn left on the highway," I said, "then it's a mile to the next turn."

He started the engine, backed to the drive, eased onto the highway and turned left.

"Beautiful day, isn't it?" I said. When someone is nice enough to give me a ride to the top, I thought, it's courteous to be a chatterbox.

He didn't answer for a minute, as though he were concentrating on the road.

"Have you ever met anybody," he said, "like the people in your books?"

My heart sank. It's not the end of the world when strangers know your name. What drives you to Celebrities Anonymous is that you're never sure whether *this particular* stranger knows it, and what might happen next. Bristle against a flower and you're a pompous fool. Embrace a spiral-eye wacko and you're hugging a land-mine.

For a hundredth of a second I considered that Shepherd might be a wacko, that I should wrench the door open and hurl myself to the highway. In the next hundredth I decided to take my chances, that I could jump later if necessary, and that diving from his car was not a fitting response to his question.

"Everybody in my books is real," I said, trusting honesty to get me through, "though some of them I've never met in spacetime."

"Is Leslie real?"

"Her favorite question." What was he getting at? The conversation was getting less innocent every minute. "You can turn off here, that's the mountain road. It's dirt and a little steep in places, but mostly a pretty easy drive. You'll want to be careful at the top, though, because paragliding's so much fun you get hooked before you drive back down, and you're never the same again."

Shepherd ignored the diversion. "The reason I ask is that I'm one of those people you write about. I was with you when you were a boy. I'm a teaching angel."

I slammed to Maximum Alert, walls up faster than light. "Enough questions," I said. "Tell me straight. What do you want?"

"It's not what I want, Richard, it's what you want."

The car was going slowly enough that I could jump

without killing myself. Still, I thought, he hadn't called me the godless antichrist, he was probably unarmed, and there remained my warm first impression. He talked like a nut-cake, but I liked the guy.

"If you're a teaching angel, you have answers," I said.

He turned to me for a moment and smiled, surprised. "Exactly! Of course I do! That's why I'm here! How did you know that?"

"I have questions," I said. "I ask, you answer, okay?" If Shepherd was a character from my books, I planned to find out.

"Of course," he said.

"I had two stuffed animals when I was a kid. What were their names?"

"Your camel is Cammie," he said, "your zebra is Zeebie."

"The first engine I made. What kind was it?" A trick question.

"It's an eighteen-inch ramjet," he said, "four-inch diameter, soldered seams, mounted on the end of a five-foot counterbalance. You know the heat's going to melt the solder and it'll blow up in a minute or two, but before it

9

does you'll see if the idea works. Alcohol for fuel. It blows up, all right. Fire all over the back yard . . ."

He talked on as he drove, describing my rockets, my house, my friends and family and dog; told fragments of my early life in detail that I didn't recall until he spoke.

The characters in my books are real, sure enough, but some are like tachyons . . . there's a dimension where they exist, each as powerful an expression of life in their worlds as we are in ours. In books they walk into my dimension and change it.

Shepherd was either one of those people or he was the world's greatest mentalist.

". . . the oleander bush by the corner of the wall. Hanging on a strut from the chimney is a mobile you made from sheet copper and welding rod. Curved ellipses—you called it *Radar*. In the garage are sheafs of charcoals and paintings, your mother's homework from her art courses. The woodbox, you use for a secret entrance to the house . . ."

"Question."

He stopped talking at once and we drove in silence, shadowed at noon by giant evergreens, the old car crunching in low gear up steep wilderness curves.

"You don't say *was,* you say *is,*" I said. "That time, my childhood. For you it still exists. The me you talk about who wants something, you mean Dickie, you mean me from my own past."

He nodded. "Of course. That time is just across the street."

"Another question."

"Ask anything."

"What's the cube of a hundred and thirty-one?"

He laughed. "I'm an angel, not a computer."

"Guess."

"Five hundred and twenty-seven?"

Wrong answer, off by millions. The guy is not omniscient, I thought, or at least math is not his gift. What else doesn't he know?

"Is there gravity in heaven?"

He turned to me surprised. "When did you think to wonder about that?"

"About a year ago. I've been . . . look out for the rock, there."

Too late. The impact brought his attention back to the road, but he drove on, divinely unconcerned. "More questions?"

I let gravity go. Right now more than heaven I needed to know this strange person.

"Why are you . . . why are you what you are?"

"We have a saying: *An excess of heart, a shortage of brain.*" The way he said the words, his proverb was sad truth.

I knew he wouldn't harm me; I knew he had found me this morning for a different purpose than a ride to the top of the mountain; I knew he was no wizard at numbers. I was filled with questions about everything else.

"And you tell me this," I said, "because it has something to do with why you are here."

"Of course."

Had I liked him on sight because I had seen that smile before?

Two

*T*eaching angels are not expert drivers. One turn on the Tiger Mountain road angles toward the edge of the cliff, and most folks hug the inside from self-preservation. Shepherd's tire-marks, however, are still there today, black rubber burned in a clutching desperate curve on bare rock.

"Sorry," he said. "I haven't driven for quite a while."

I braced my feet and gripped the ragged armrest. "It eases up in a bit."

Hard or easy didn't matter to my driver; he had a different agenda. "You don't remember much about yourself when you were little, do you?"

"When you tell me, I remember. Otherwise, not much."

"You're a fine boy. When you want to learn something, you are very serious about it. Remember learning to write?"

I thought of John Gartner's creative writing class in high school. Does anybody learn writing, or do they just touch someone who lets them see the power of the deleted word?

"No," he said. "Handwriting. Your mother at the kitchen table, writing letters, you sitting alongside with pencil and paper, drawing O's and L's and E's, loops and curves and rounds, page after page."

I remembered. Red pencil. And R's and S's. It felt so grown-up, to be making those orderly marks left to right across the paper. Mom said it was beautiful work, made me want to practice all the more. Today I have the worst hand-writing in the world.

"So you know Dickie pretty well, do you?" I said.

He nodded. "A whole lot better than I know you."

"Because he needs help and I don't?"

"Because he wants help and you don't."

The Ford turned a last curve and we reached the top of the mountain, trees giving way to sudden wide horizons opened north and west. He parked within a hundred feet of the paraglider launch, and I reached to open my door.

"I'm glad you're there for him," I said. "Give him my regards, will you?"

He didn't respond. I got out of the car, lifted my paraglider pack from the rear seat, slung it on my shoulder. The wind was as light as before. Unless I can soar this time, I thought, it'll be one last hop, then pack up and go home.

I leaned down and waved to him through the window. "Pleasure to meet you, Mr. Shepherd," I said. "Thanks for the ride."

He nodded, and I started to move away. "Oh, just one thing," he said.

I turned back.

"Would you mind signing a book for Dickie?"

"Not at all." That such a thing was impossible didn't occur to me. What leaps the fence of time is hope and intuition, not packages of paper and ink.

I set the pack on the ground, opened the door, slid again into the car.

Shepherd touched the book between us on the front

seat. "You made a promise," he said. "You probably don't remember."

"You're right. I don't remember." As a kid I was full of fantasies: wishes and dreams, designs for the way things ought to be. I wouldn't be surprised if some of my dreams I remember as fact, and some of the facts I remember as dreams.

"That was long ago, Mr. Shepherd. Dickie's so distant now he's a different person, I've forgotten who he was."

"Well, you're not a different person to him. He thinks you'll never forget him, that you'll do anything to help him learn how to live. He's desperate to find what you know."

"He'll find it," I said.

"But by then he'll be your age. You promised an experiment, to see what he'd become if he didn't have to spend fifty years at trial and error."

"I promised myself?"

Shepherd nodded. "In 1944, when I told you that time was not the wall for me that it was for you. You promised that in fifty years you'd write a book to take back, just for the boy you were, everything you know. What to look out for, how to be happy, knowledge to save your life, things you wish you'd known when you were him."

16

"No. Really?" The wind-streamers ruffled in a thermal cresting the mountaintop. "What a sweet idea."

Shepherd cleared his throat. "It's fifty years later, Richard." He shifted, uncomfortable in his seat. "He's waiting back there, the boy that you were. You promised."

"I don't remember any promise."

The angel looked at me as though I had sold my soul. The words had come out a little harsh, I thought, but neither boy nor angel knows how hard it is to write. "Tell him I forgot the promise, but that everything is going to work out all right and he's not to worry."

Shepherd sighed. "Ah, Richard," he said. "Do promises to children mean nothing to you?"

"Not when keeping them is going to break their heart! He doesn't want to know there are storms ahead, that before long he'll be the only one of his family left alive, he doesn't want to know about divorce and betrayal and bankruptcy, that he won't marry the woman of his heart for another thirty-five years. Shepherd, *one* year is forever to a nine-year-old. You're right, that promise means nothing!"

"I thought you might feel that way," he said. A sad smile. "I do know how hard it is to write a book. I knew you wouldn't write it, so I did it for you."

Three

"All you need to do is sign it," the angel said, handing me the book. "It'll be our secret, that you didn't have time to do the writing yourself. Dickie never has to know. He thinks you're God, no matter what."

"There will be no lying to the little guy," I said. "You tell him straight: he has no idea what he's asking. Tell him I said that he will know when he's my age that books aren't written on whims or old promises. Books are written on years turned inside out by ideas that never let go until you get them in print, and even then writing's a last resort, a desperate ransom you pay to get your life back. Wonderful when it's over and everything I ever had to say I have already written, thank the Maker, and I now have earned an afternoon on the mountaintop with my paraglider!"

"I'll tell him what I have to tell him," he said, not much dismayed. "And of course I know what you'd write. Just sign the book, not that you wrote it, maybe, but that you endorse it, that you know it's true. Then I'll go." He pulled a felt-tip pen from his pocket. "Just a word of encouragement: *Have faith!* and a signature."

For the first time, I looked at the volume he had handed me. A forest-green cover, white block title. *ANSWERS— Some Directions for What to Do and Think in Order to Live a Successful Life. Results Guaranteed* by Richard Bach.

My heart sank. Still, I thought, a lot of good books have really dumb titles.

I opened the cover, looked at the table of contents.

> *Family*
> *School*
> *Study*
> *Going to Work*
> *Money*
> *Responsibility*
> *Obligations*
> *Service*
> *Caring for others*

It went on, two pages in small print just to name the chapters. If Dickie has any problem getting to sleep, I thought, his troubles will soon be over.

I opened the book at random. *An important part of your*

work environment is the provision for employment benefits. A good retirement plan is as good as a higher salary, and an automatic cost-of-living adjustment is the same as money in the bank.

Grf, I thought. What about finding what you love to do, and letting that be your business?

Try again. *Everything you do reflects on your family. Before you do anything that might embarrass them, think: Will my family be happy if I'm caught doing this?*

Oh, my. Third time's got to be the winner. *God's watching. Time will come He'll ask: Were you a good citizen? Tell Him that at least you tried.*

I swallowed, suddenly nervous, turned pages. The kid wants to know what I've learned in fifty years, and he gets this? How can an angel write such hellish ideas?

You create your own reality, so be sure to create a happy one. Sacrifice yourself for others, and they will be nice to you.

I was surprised at how hard it was to tear the book in two, but when I managed that I thrust one of the wrecked halves in front of Shepherd's face. "*You create your own reality? They'll be nice to you?* I can't figure whether you're insane to believe that or insane to think I do! Either way you are crazy putting this in a book for an innocent child . . . for Dickie! to read! Reality is what he sees with his eyes? What kind of diabolical . . . dragon-master are you working for?"

I stopped because I couldn't make my voice go any higher, and noticed that my hand trembled as it clutched the pages an inch from the angel's nose.

"It's not set in concrete," he offered. "I can change it, if you want . . ."

"Shepherd, the little guy had a *dream!* He had a grand idea, to find what life he'd live if he didn't have to spend half a century sifting truth from lies! You take his dream and you turn it to *employment benefits?* And you're going to tell him it's from *me?"*

"You did promise," he said, his voice the soul of righteousness. "I knew you didn't care enough to write the book. I was trying to make it easy for you."

I was swept down a river of rage, signs on the shore: *Danger. Falls Ahead.* What falls? How could I possibly be more furious than I was this minute? Was I going to strangle this creature with my bare hands?

All at once my voice went very quiet. "Shepherd, you are free to do anything you wish to do. But if you give to that innocent child this mass of vapid slurry and call it a half-century's learning with my name on it" [here my eyes may have glowed, needle-tips of white-hot daggers], "I will track you to hell and stuff you with it, page by page."

It wasn't the threat that reached him, I think, but my earnest resolve.

"Well," he said. "I'm glad you care."

That's what it takes to be an angel—they always see the bright side.

Four

I lifted my pack and stalked away, shaking my head. Another lesson learned, I thought. Just because somebody drops in on you from another dimension, Richard, don't assume they're wiser than you about anything at all, or that they can do anything better than you can do yourself. Discarnate or mortal, what matters about people is *the quality of what they've learned*.

I unfolded the wing on the mountaintop for launch, grumbling about vacubrain angels meddling in my past. When I looked up, the Ford and its strange driver had disappeared.

I prayed that Shepherd had vanished, instead of attempting the drive down. If he chose the drive, I expected I'd find him off the road in some tree-branch next time I came up the mountain.

Harness on, gloves on, buckles and helmet checked and secure. The other paragliders had long since launched and three had landed. Three wings were still aloft, down low, butterflies over evergreen, whistling for lift.

Lacking breeze to kite the wing before launch, I lunged straight toward the cliff, looked up to check my big rainbow smoothly overhead, ran ahead into the air.

Wouldn't Dickie love to be flying with me now . . . this could show him what's important in a lifetime! You find what you love and you learn everything about it. You bet your life on what you know and you run from safety, off your mountain into the air, trusting the Principle of Flight to bring you soaring up on lift you cannot see with your eyes.

At that moment, a comma to my thought, the wing caught a rising current of air. I pulled the right brake handle down, turning to stay with the thermal, and the rainbow and I lifted softly skyward.

Over the hills west raised the distant skyline of Seattle, glittering Emerald City in late-century Oz. Sunlight sparkled on Puget Sound, and beyond, the Olympic Mountains kept cool under hats of snow. There's a lot in this moment he'd love to see.

A moth appeared not ten feet to my right, flapping her little wings resolutely, flying just as fast as I. I turned toward her and she angled away, then reversed toward me, roared past my helmet and disappeared southward.

Is that something Dickie would know, he who loved airborne things, what a moth was doing flying south at two thousand feet?

After all, I thought, the child I was didn't live in Shepherd's thought, he lived in mine. So little of my childhood I remembered, and Dickie holds it all. My motives and values sprang every one from roots in his daily life. If I found a way to reach him, I might learn something myself, as well as teach him a lot about trials and errors yet to come.

The lift died away—in minutes Seattle descended once more behind the hills. The first of the paragliders to land was already back at the launch site, watching me below, gliding down.

If I relaxed, here in midair, I thought, invite the door to open between me and the child I was, what would happen? It's been so long since I've even thought about the lad! Had it not been for Shepherd and his book of lies I wouldn't have thought about Dickie at all.

I imagined a door deep into my past, lifted the heavy wooden latch, creaked it open. Dark inside, and cold— that's a surprise. Maybe he's sleeping.

"Dickie," I called in my mind, "it's me, Richard. It's been fifty years, little guy! Want to say hello?"

He was waiting for me in the dark, pointing a flame-thrower. Tenth of a second, and the place lit up with fire and scarlet fury. "OUT! GET THE GOD-DARN HECK OUT OF HERE YOU CARELESS SELFISH MISERA-BLE SO-CALLED GROWN-UP HATEFUL PERSON I HOPE I NEVER TURN INTO! GET OUT AND NEVER COME BACK AND *LEAVE ME ALONE!*"

I gasped, shuddered back in my helmet, slammed the door shut, woke up fast to the harness and wing above the trees of Tiger Mountain.

Whuf! I thought. Is my mind loading rockets for me? Here I was expecting the little guy to come running to my arms, from darkness into light, full of questions, open for all the wisdom I have to give. I unlock the door to a won-derful new friendship and no warning he nearly fries me alive!

So much for loving our inner child. Lucky that door's got a big heavy latch. Never will I even walk near this place, let alone touch that trigger-bomb again.

By the time I landed, the other paragliders were set to launch once more, wind or not. Just as well, I thought. I packed the wing, set it in the trunk of my car, started the

26

engine and all the way home I thought about what had happened.

Leslie waved from a plum tree when I arrived, pruning shears in her hand, uneven branch-tips littering the ground below.

"Hi, sweetie," she called. "Did you have a good flight? Did you have fun?"

My wife is a loving and beautiful woman, the soulmate found after I had given up searching. If only she could be these things but for once not quite so deep and mysterious and challenging. *Did you have fun?* How could I answer that question?

Five

"*A flamethrower?*" Anyone else would have laughed, her husband come home to tell such a story. She curled into the couch beside me, blanket over her feet, a cup of mint tea cradled to warm her hands. If one has to get cold-soaked, she believes, pruning trees in springtime is the best way to do it.

"What does a flamethrower mean to you?"

"It means I'm upset," I said. "I want to obliterate somebody. Not just kill them, but change them mostly to ashes."

"If that's what happens when you're upset," she said, "what goes on when you're really mad?"

"All right, Leslie. He wasn't just upset, he was really mad."

By the time I told her the story, I had changed it from disturbing into funny. Shepherd was a wacko fanatic, read something in a book that fixed his mind on me, invented this story, wrote his awful manuscript and hoped I'd get it published for him.

Was he a teaching angel? We're all teaching angels, we've all learned something that someone somewhere needs to remember. I should have told him straight off that I didn't have my learning-cap on today, and that I planned to hike to the top of the mountain thank you very much good day.

My wife didn't smile so easily about the encounter with the child that I had been. She had long suspected the boy was a living part of me, abandoned, needing to be found and loved. In Shepherd she had found an ally.

"Can you imagine any reason in the world why Dickie might be mad at you?"

"It was dark and cold down there, it was a cell in a dungeon," I told her. "If he thought I locked him in there, just walked away and left him helpless in the dark . . ." I considered the feeling. "I can imagine he might be a little annoyed."

"Annoyed?" She frowned at me.

"Okay. I can imagine he'd like to cut me into little tiny bits and feed me to rats."

"Is he right? Are you the one that locked the door?"

I lay my head back on her shoulder, sighed at the rafters. "Am I supposed to bring him along? Every week there's a new gang of people I used to be, added to all the ones who came before. Tomorrow I'm going to be one of them, my-self. Does the current-me have to drag this crowd around with him, careful don't hurt their feelings, take a vote what do we do now?" Even to me I sounded defensive.

"Not the crowd," she said. "But if you push them all away, not even a memory from your childhood, do you have a past at all?"

"I've got memories." I pouted, and knew she heard the unsaid rest: so few times I recall, sparse greentree oases in the lifewide wilderness of childhood. Ought to be a won-derland, I thought, but it's vacant when I look back, as if I've dropped in, visitor to Now snuck through on a fake pastport.

"Tell me a hundred memories," she said.

Leslie's past has its own black holes, foster homes turned empty static in her mind, no recollection of a little girl's injuries showing clear on sheets of X rays. Yet her daily life is rich with memory of the child she was, old knowing helping her decide today and choose tomorrow.

"Settle for two?"

"Okay, two," she said.

"I forget."

"Come on. You can remember if you want to."

"Watching clouds. Lying on my back, hidden in an empty lot by my house, wild wheat green around me. Looking up to the sky was looking up through an impossible deep sea, the clouds were islands, floating."

"Okay," she said. "Watching clouds. Next?"

But that's important, I thought. Don't brush away watching clouds, the sky was my escape, it was my love, it turned out to be my future and it's still my future now. Don't say next, the sky meant everything!

"The water tower," I said.

"What's the water tower?"

"We lived in Arizona when I was little. On a ranch that had a water tower."

"What was it about the water tower? Why do you remember?"

"I don't know," I said. "It was the biggest thing around, I guess."

"Okay. Next memory?"

"That's two."

She waited a long time, as though she were expecting three after I had told her not a hundred memories but two.

"I spent an afternoon in a tree, once, till just about dark," I said. There, I thought. I gave her more than I promised.

"Why were you in a tree?"

"I don't know. You wanted memories, not reasons."

More silence. A few other images wrenched through inner focus on the jerky wobbling reel I called my childhood, but like the tree and the water tower they were monuments to nothing: a bicycle ride with a childhood friend; a tiny sculpture of a laughing Buddha. If I told her and if she asked what they meant, I'd be lost to explain.

"Three of my grandparents died before I was born, the last when I was little. And my brother died then, too. But you know that." Statistics, I thought, not memories.

Leslie had been devastated by her own brother's death, refused to believe I hadn't been crushed when mine died. But the truth was that I had barely noticed. "That's about it."

I expected she'd bring it up again: How can your *brother* die and you call it a statistic not even a memory?

"Do you remember telling Dickie you'd write him a book?"

Her words were so even I guessed she was hatching some theme. Nothing that happened today, I thought, is end-of-the-world material. The scariest part, the kid with the flamethrower, was all in my mind.

"Don't be silly," I said. "How would I remember such a thing?"

"Pretend, Richie. Pretend you're nine years old again. Grandma and Grandpa Shaw are dead, Grandma and Grandpa Bach are dead, your brother Bobby's just died. Who's next? Aren't you scared that tomorrow you'll be dead, too? Don't you worry about the future? What are you *feeling*?"

What was she trying to say? She knows I don't worry. If there's a threat, I'll dodge if I can. If I can't, I take it head-on. You either plan for what's ahead or you fight with what you've got; worry is a waste of time.

But for her sake I closed my eyes and pretended I was there, watching the nine-year-old, knowing what he thought.

I found him at once, frozen on his bed, eyes slammed shut, fists clenched, alone. He wasn't worried, he was terrified.

"If Bobby with his lightning mind can't find a way past age eleven, then I don't have a prayer," I said to Leslie as I saw. "I know it doesn't make sense, but I know I'm going to die when I'm ten."

What a queer feeling, to stand in my old room again! The bunkbed by the window, upper bunk still there after Bobby's death; the white pine desk, its top marred by Testor's Extra-Fast Drying Cement and X-Acto blades; balsa-rib paper-covered Comet flying models hanging on threads from the ceiling; painted-wood Strombecker solid models perched on shelves among the books, each made from hours all at once remembered: a JU-88 Stuka in brown, a Piper Cub in yellow, a Lockheed P-38, one of its twin tails cracked from a launch off the top bunk . . . I had forgotten there were so many little airplanes in my childhood. A cast metal P-40 and an FW-190, both in crude detail, parked on the desk by the gooseneck lamp.

"Look at this room," I said. "How can I remember so clearly? All these years it's been fog!"

Over the closet were two cabinet doors. Inside, I knew, lay the Monopoly set, the Ouija board, Cammie and Zeebie, winter blankets. Careful on the old braided rag rug over the hardwood floor, it'll slip like ice from under unless you tread really slow.

"Do you want to talk to him?" said Leslie.

"No. I'm just observing." Why should it frighten me to talk with him?

He was wearing jeans and a plaid flannel longsleeve shirt, black squares on dark red, faint yellow pinstripes crossing.

What a young face! A band of freckles across the nose and cheekbones; hair lighter than mine, skin darker, from hours in the sun. Face wider and rounder, tears streaking from eyes clamped shut. A good-looking kid, scared to death.

Oh, come on, Dickie, I thought. It's going to be all right.

All at once his eyes flew open, he saw me watching and opened his mouth to scream.

I slammed by reflex back to modern times, the boy vanishing for me in the same instant that I must have vanished for him.

"Hello!" I said, way too late.

Six

"Hello what?" said Leslie.

"Just silly," I told her. "He saw me."

"What did he say?"

"Nothing. We were both pretty startled. What an odd thing."

"How do you feel about him?"

"He'll be okay. He just doesn't know what comes next, and he's scared."

"How do you feel about him?"

"Everything's going to be all right. He's going to do well in school, he's going to have a great time learning all sorts of things: airplanes, astronomy, rockets, sailing, div-ing . . ."

She touched my hand. "How do you feel about him?"

"It broke my heart! I wish to God I could pick him up and hug him and tell him don't cry you're safe you're not going to die!"

Dear Leslie, my love and deepest friend. She didn't say a word. She let me listen to what I had said, in silence, over and over.

I scrambled for balance. I've never been much on feelings, being as how they are private property and often best suppressed. A tall order to suppress, I thought, but not impossible. The whole thing, after all, is only in my head.

"You're the keeper of his future," she said into the quiet.

"His most probable future," I said. "He has others."

"You're the one who knows what he needs to know. If ever his life is going to fly higher than yours, you're the one to tell him how."

In that moment, I did love the little guy. And when I was with him, my childhood wasn't fog, it was crystal, nothing lost.

"I'm the keeper of his future," I said, "he's the keeper of my past."

In that moment I had the strangest feeling that they needed each other, Dickie and Richard, if each were ever to be whole. Did I have to go alone, me the retreater, to meet a child who hated me to ashes, to show him personally that I loved him, no matter what? I would rather crawl to Oregon through broken glass.

What other way? My bent reels kept blurred monochrome footage of the time from which I had come, faded question marks; Dickie strode mural corridors of sunlight color, details etched in finepoint, nothing missing.

Still he trembled over darkness to come, no matter how clearly I knew the dark was the shadow of adventures ahead, discovery sweeping down to pick him up and teach what he begged to know.

Lean into your fears, I wished I could tell him, dare them to do their worst and cut them down when they try. If you don't, they'll clone themselves, Dickie, they'll mushroom till they surround you, choke the road to the life you want. Every turn you fear is empty air, dressed to look like jagged hell.

Easy for me to say; I'd lived through them all. Not so easy for him.

If I'm afraid today, I thought, what do I most wish to hear from the wise and future me?

When the time comes to fight, Richard, I will be with
you, and the weapon you need will be in your hand.

Could I say that for him now, with the faintest hope
he'd understand?

Not likely, I thought, when I'm the one he wants to
fight.

Seven

"*L*eslie, why don't I just forget the whole thing? I have a lot better things to do with my life than to play with my own imagination."

"Right you are," she said, stretching luxuriously. "How about rice for dinner?"

"No, I mean really. What do I possibly have to gain from closing my eyes and pretending I'm friends with a little person who owns my childhood? What do I care about ancient history?"

"It's not ancient history, it's now," she said. "You know who you are, he knows why. If you're friends, you can trade. But nobody says you have to do anything. I love you the way you are."

I hugged her for that. "Thank you, sweetie."

"Doesn't bother me," she said. "I don't care if you're a spineless coward, afraid to admit you've got any hint of feeling or caring or any other human emotion, that you don't realize you ever were a child, think you're some walk-in from outer space. You're a good cook, and that's what matters in a husband."

Oh, my, I thought. She thinks it'll be Good for Me, to go back and open that Pandora-door to Dickie's cell. Another woman would say she'd never want no husband of hers to go mucking about who knows how long in the dark of his mind, trying to be friends with a make-believe child.

Children have imaginary adults for friends, I thought, can adults have imaginary children for theirs? In my own books, I thought, Jonathan Seagull is imaginary, and Donald Shimoda and Pye . . . three of my four closest friends and dearest teachers don't have bodies. What are the odds that Dickie might change my life as well?

I'm losing control here, I thought, thanks to mad Shepherd and his screwy fantasies. If ever I see that old Ford again, I'll write the license number first thing, find out what kind of previous convictions that guy's hiding. How can a wacko turn my ordered life into a cuckoo clock?

"Rice it is," I said at last.

I left Leslie on the couch with her cool teacup, put the

wok on the stove, added flames, a little olive oil, pulled celery and onions and peppers and ginger from the fridge and chopped them fine.

What am I so afraid of? Who's running my mind, after all? I'll just imagine the little guy a lot nicer to me this time . . . he can come to me with an apology for the flame-thrower, fill in the blanks about my childhood then go his separate imaginary way, pretend happier, pretend wiser, nobody's the worse for meeting.

In flew the diced vegetables, yesterday's rice sizzling after, a swirl of soy, a bean sprout, two.

If it's so much fun for me to set new physical records, I thought—jog the mile in ten minutes instead of 10:35, stay aloft in the paraglider for two and a half hours instead of two and a quarter—if I push myself to widen my physical envelope, what's wrong with pushing my emotional envelope as well?

I set plates on the table, blue on white, with painted flowers to match the real ones Leslie picks fresh for the house.

I don't have to do it, I thought, nobody's forcing me. But if I'm curious to know what I left back there in my childhood and how finding it might change me today, is that some kind of crime? Are the Macho Police going to pound on my door, arrest me for not being cool? Anybody dare tell me I can't walk through my own past, for the fun of it?

"Dinnertime, Wookie," I called.

Over the meal we talked about children, of all things. I told her how proud I was of mine for making the choices they had, how glad I was not to be a child again myself, not to face again the toughest cruelest weakest lostest years most people ever live.

"You're right," Leslie said, as I got us each a strawberry for dessert. "It's a shame that any child has to go through that time alone."

Eight

I never can't sleep. Kiss my wife goodnight, pound a hole in the pillow, fall down into it and by the time my head touches bottom I'm gone.

Not tonight. Two hours after Leslie was off in her dreams, I stared at the ceiling yet, living the day through for the thirteenth time.

Last I looked at the clock, it was one a.m., six hours from sunup. Come noon I'll be out to tinker a bit with Daisy, our Cessna Skymaster.

Hope it's raining tomorrow, I thought in the dark. I need to fly some weather approaches, keep the rust off my instrument rating. To Bayview to shoot the nondirectional beacon approach there, pop over to Port Angeles for the ILS . . .

Anywhere but sleep, I thought.

Afraid Dickie's going to torch his way through the door and flame you in your bed?

This is silly! What am I afraid of? When Leslie's angry with me, do I still run away? Of course. Not as much as I used to. Then why am I running from that wooden cell? I did shut him away there, it was wrong and I'm sorry I can't imagine what I was doing. It was not a deliberate act and the least I can do is open the door and let him out, the little imaginary guy.

In half an hour, on the edge of sleep, I saw the door again, cold and dark as ever.

Lean into my fears, I thought, dare them do their worst and cut them down when they try. Every turn I fear is empty air, dressed to look like hell.

I lifted the bolt, but held the door closed.

"Dickie, it's me, Richard. I didn't know what I was doing. I was wrong. I'm terribly sorry for what I did."

I heard him move, inside. "Good!" he said. "Now you step in here and let me lock the door on you for fifty years. After that I'll come back and tell you how sorry I am. See how you feel about that. Fair's darn fair, yeah?"

45

I opened the door. "Fair's fair," I said. "I'm sorry. I was a fool, cutting you off. My life's poorer for what I did. Now it's your turn. Lock me up."

The blue primer-fire at the muzzle of his flamethrower flickered at me, pointed at my face the moment I opened the door. No matter what, I thought, I won't run away. It is his freedom to kill me if he wants.

He didn't move from his seat on the bench opposite the door.

"You locked me in here and you *left me alone*! You didn't care if I screamed or cried, you didn't hear you didn't care," he said. "RICHARD, I COULD HAVE HELPED YOU! I could have helped you and you didn't want me, you didn't love me, you didn't even CARE!"

"I came back to say I'm sorry," I said. "I'm the biggest dumbest idiot in the world."

"You think just because I live in your mind I don't matter I don't hurt I don't need you to protect me and teach me and love me, WELL, I DO! You think I'm not real I'm not living I'm not scared of what you'll do to me, WELL, I AM!"

"I don't know much about caring, Dickie. When I locked you in here, I locked a lot of my feelings in with you, I've been out there in the world running mostly on intellect. I didn't know you were here till yesterday, and I came right away." My eyes opened to the dark. "You scare me this minute as much as I scare you. You've got every right to torch me off. Before you do, I want you to know I saw you lying on the bed, just after Bobby died. I wanted to tell you everything's going to be all right. I wanted to tell you I love you."

His eyes blazed, darker than the night of his cell. "This is how you love me? Lock me away? Keep me from being a part of your life? I lived the hard times for you, I DE-SERVE to know what you know, and I DON'T! YOU LOCKED ME UP! NOT EVEN WINDOWS, YOU LOCKED ME UP! DO YOU KNOW WHAT THAT FEELS LIKE?"

"No."

"It feels like a diamond in a safe! It feels like a butterfly in chains! It feels life-less! Do you know *life-less*? Do you know cold? Do you know dark? Do you know someone who ought to love you more than anyone in the world and they don't care whether you live or die?"

"I know lonely," I said.

"Lonely, heck! Try somebody you love, try me grabbing you against your will and sticking you in a shut wooden cage and slamming a big lock down over the door and leaving you there no food no water no hello for fifty years!

Try that and tell me you're sorry! I hate you! If there's anything I have to give to you, anything you need from me, anything you'll die without, let me starve you for it till the day you drop and then tell me you're sorry! *I HATE YOU'RE SORRY!*"

All I had was reason, the only weapon in my hand. "This minute, Dickie, it's the first of a million minutes we can spend together if there's anything you want from being together. I don't know how many minutes we have, you and I. You can torch me, you can lock me in here and walk out for the rest of our lives, and if that'll balance my cruelty to you, let's do it. But I've got a lot to show you about how I think the world works. You want to know right now what you'll learn in fifty years? That's me, standing right in front of you. Half a century trial mostly error but now and then I've stumbled over true, too. Lock me away if you want, or use me to make your old dreams happen. Your choice."

"I hate you," he said.

"You have every right to hate me. Is there any way I can make it up to you? Is there anything you've dreamed about, that I can show you? If I've done it, if I've lived it, if I know it, it's yours."

He looked at me in the gloom, he turned the flame-thrower away and his dark eyes filled with tears.

"Oh, Richard," he said. "What's it like to fly?"

Nine

*L*eslie listened to the story straight through come morning, and when I finished she sat in bed, watching her flower garden outside the windows, silent as thought.

"You left a lot behind, Richie. Didn't you ever look back?"

"Not many of us do, I don't think. Childhood was not something I was much trained to treasure. The point was to get through it. Learn as much as you can along the way, but hunch in, hold your breath, coast down that long powerless hill of dependence till you're rolling fast enough to pop the clutch and start your engine on your own."

"You were nine when your brother died?"

"About," I said. "What's that got to do with it?"

49

"Dickie's nine," she said.

I nodded.

"It was pretty hard for you, wasn't it?"

"Nope. Bobby's death didn't affect me. Isn't that strange? I feel like I ought to lie to you, tell you that was a tough one, all right. But it wasn't, Wookie. He went to the hospital, he died, and the rest of us went on with our business. Nobody cried, that I saw. No point in crying when there's nothing you can do."

"Most people would have been devastated."

"Why? Do we grieve when somebody walks out of sight? They're as alive as we are, but because we can't see them we're supposed to grieve? It doesn't make a lot of sense. If we're eternal creatures . . ."

"Did you think you were an eternal creature at age nine? Did you think Bobby was just walking out of sight when he died?"

"I don't remember. But that is a deep intuition. I wouldn't be surprised."

"I would. I think you found a lot of that intuition after your brother went to the hospital and never came back."

"Maybe so," I said. "My notes were lost."

She turned to me, wide blue eyes. "You kept *notes*? When your brother . . ."

"Just kidding, sweetie. I didn't keep notes. I barely remember he died at all."

She didn't smile. "Dickie remembers, I'll bet."

"I'm not sure I want to know. Right now I'd just like to make peace with him and move on."

"Shut him away again?"

I lay back in bed, studied the grain in the wood planks overhead, the knot that looks like a spider clinging by its little toes to the edge. No, not shut anybody away.

"What did he mean, Leslie: *I could have helped you*?"

"When you go flying," she said. "Let's say it's a beautiful day and you want to fly, just for the fun of it. Do you go out to the airport and buy a ticket to be a passenger in the back-back seat of the biggest heaviest steeliest monster jet transport you can find?"

I hadn't the least idea where she was taking me. "Nope. I take the paraglider to the mountain or I roll Daisy out of her hangar and I pick the prettiest part of the sky and I

51

melt into the wing and then into the air, till I'm just soul on a sunbeam. There is probably a reason why you asked."

"Remember your way around problems when you can't run away from them?"

"Is there another way? Cram the gears to low," I said, "stomp the throttle to the floor, close my eyes tight, four miles an hour, and drive straight on through."

"Do you think what Dickie meant when he said *I could have helped you* is that if you found a way to make him your friend, you could open your eyes?"

Ten

Settling myself in Daisy's cockpit with Dickie in my mind felt like being a kid again myself. The boy I had been was no more my sudden friend than some wild raccoon rescued from a leg-hold trap, but as he saw the airplane through my eyes for the first time, I saw it through his, his voice in my head.

"Wow! Look at all the dials and knobs! What's this?"

"That's the altitude indicator," I said. "See the little airplane there? That's us and there's the little horizon, so when we're in the clouds we know we're . . ."

"What are these?"

"These are propeller pitch controls, one for each engine. We set them forward for takeoff and then in cruise we . . ."

53

"What's *that*?"

"That shows where lightning is, on stormy days. So we know where not to fly."

"Let me turn the wheel!"

I smiled, at that. It felt like touching a control wheel for the first time in my life, heavy but easy to turn. All business, that wheel, all delight.

"What are the buttons?"

"Here's the microphone button. Here's the trim switch. Here's the speed-brakes, the autopilot disconnect, these are the moving-map controls . . ."

"Make the engines start!"

I pushed the mixtures full rich.

"Can I do it?"

What did it feel like, to the child within me? To sit in the pilot's seat of a real airplane for the first time, and *already know how to make it work*? Heaven!

Battery master switch on, boost pump on for the front engine.

"CLEAR THE FRONT PROP!" I called. Magneto switch to START, and . . . Holy Cats, listen to that engine light up!

Tumbling hollow firecrackers; our own thunderstorm.

I had forgotten the way an airplane shivers and dances, that second the engine starts, as if she can't believe she's alive again, and going to fly.

"CLEAR THE REAR PROP!" Magneto switch to START.

TWO thunderstorms!

He pointed to any gauge that moved, I answered his finger's questions.

"Tachometers! Oil pressures! Fuel flows! Exhaust gas temps!"

How long I had flown, how many years, without drinking as he did the delight of every moment in this cockpit? Calm deep pleasure, it had been; oh, so grown-up.

"Hark!" I said, and pressed the radio select button for the airport traffic information. Hark? I thought.

". . . wind one seven zero degrees at one five knots," said the voice in the headset, "arriving and departing runway one six right, advise on initial contact that you have information Kilo . . ."

I pressed the microphone button and he went wild. He was talking to a *control tower*!

"Hi, Ground, Skymaster One Four Four Four Alpha, out of the west hangars with Kilo . . ." He was the spirit behind my voice, talking just the way a real pilot would talk, and he was beside himself.

"Neat-O!" he said when we taxied into position for takeoff. For the first time he realized that he didn't have a little boy's body anymore. He could reach the throttles and the rudder pedals without having to stuff cushions all around, he could see over the glareshield and watch the runway just like a real pilot!

Pushing those throttles forward was the first time in his life he touched big power. Thunderstorms turned tornadoes, Daisy lunged ahead, pressing us back in the seat in her rush to get to the sky.

The runway center-stripe changed from slow white dashes to a seventy-mile lightning-blur beneath us.

"Up! Up! Up!"

He tugged on the control wheel, the airplane tilted her

nose upward and we climbed, a snow-and-lemon rocket fired into the sky.

"Wheels up! Flaps up!" he cried. "Go, Daisy! Go! Go!"

To me the climb was sixteen hundred feet a minute, I could read that on the vertical speed indicator. To him it was somebody cut the chains, the ground fell away like a piano and we were out the top into empty space. Free at last!

I turned us away from the airport, off-airways, out of air-traffic-control country, he banked us toward a grand cumulus island floating near the mountains. Better than dreams, better a million than lying in the weeds and pretending he's on that cloud.

By the time we hit the cumulus we were flying something over 220 miles per hour, all the thrill of flying into solid white marble without annoying death to take the fun away.

"Wow! WOW! *WOW!*"

A bumpy ride, inside the cloud, but at that speed not for long. We shot out the other side a white-hot fireball, spirals of mist trailing from our wingtips.

"Holy CATS!"

We turned back, climbed the snow-tower past its top, banked steep to gaze down at the boiling peak that no one in the world had seen before or would see again, then flew past the sheer slope, extreme skiers seven thousand feet midair, plunged off the edge.

"GO, DAISY!!"

Unbelievable, I thought. He's a little kid!

"Over the mountains!" he said. "Where nobody's ever climbed!"

I kept us legal and safe, gliding range to a forced-landing place should both engines fail, one eye for fuel quantity, for oil pressure and engine temperatures.

He looked through the windshield and made Daisy fly.

Below us, mountain lakes lofted above timberline, melted bright cobalt from high snowfields. Not a road, not a hiking trail, not a tree. Razor spires of sudden granite, vast stone plates and bowls overflowed in snowflakes, sky-color riverlets throwing themselves wild abandon into empty air.

"A BEAR! Richard, Looklooklook! A BEAR!"

I knew that bears for sure have no business up so high in the mountains, then caught that for grown-up thinking, squashing everything into reasons, ignoring grizzlies just below.

The bear stood on her hind feet, sniffing at us, I guess, as we whirled toward her.

"Dickie, you're right as rain! A bear!"

"She's waving!"

He rocked our wings to wave back, and in the next second we flashed over the mountaincrest, diving for the valley, me and the kid I used to be, the one who never had a chance to fly.

An hour later, landed and taxied back to the hangar, Dickie split away from me and I saw him in his own body again, eager to get out of the cockpit and look at Daisy from the outside. He opened the door, jumped down and ran his hands over the airplane, as though studying her from a foot away wasn't enough.

I stepped to the ground, watched him for a minute. "What do you see?"

"This very metal," he said, "this very paint has been *inside a cloud*! It's been *above the highest mountain*! It has been! Feel it yourself!"

It was as if magic clung still to Daisy's skin, and he wasn't going to let a drop get away. I felt it, too.

"Thank you, Daisy," I said, courteous old habit.

Dickie ran to the front of the airplane, threw his arms around the front-engine propeller and kissed the bright spinner. "Thank you, Daisy," he said, "for a wonderful beautiful happy high beautiful wonderful wonderful wonderful ride you beautiful big sleek fast wonderful airplane I love you!"

What did I care if there were fingerprints and kiss-marks on Daisy's clean paint? I had remembered what it is to fly!

Eleven

When I came home, Leslie was at her computer, working late. I stopped at her office door and she looked up, smiled. "Hi, Wook. How was the flight with Dickie?"

"Fine," I said. "Very interesting." I set my flight bag by the door, draped my jacket on the chair, scanned the mail. Why was it so hard to tell her the excitement of the airplane ride?

"Every flight is interesting," she said. "What's wrong?"

"Nothing. It's just so . . . childish, I guess, I feel like a fool, talking about it."

"Richard, it's supposed to be childish!" she said. "You are inviting a child into your mind, where one has never been!"

"You won't think I'm crazy, if I tell you?"

"I've always thought you were crazy," she said. "Don't make me change."

I laughed, told her what had happened, how it felt to think like a kid again, everything new as if I had never flown before, felt it all for the first time.

"Wonderful, sweetie," she said. "How many people could have done what you did today? I'm proud of you!"

"But it can't go on forever. What happens when I want to tell him about grown-up things, does he care? Women, marriage, earning a living, building a religion—there's nothing more interesting and I'm scared he's going to yawn in the middle and want a candy bar. I don't know children, I don't have anything to say to children till they're grown-up."

"Could he be what you used to say about yourself," she asked, "absolutely ignorant but infinitely intelligent? If he hopes you write him a book of everything you've learned in fifty years, he probably wants more than candy bars."

I nodded, remembered when I was him . . . I needed to know everything about everything except business, government and medicine, and I needed to know it now.

I puzzled over that for a moment, why the exceptions?

They're dull for me today because each turns around social contracts, and there's nothing so boring as consensus with reluctant others. He must have felt the same. Could we have more in common than a past, could we share some core values yet unfound? How did he shape the person I became? What could his values be?

I stared at the carpet. A nine-year-old with values? Let us not get carried away, here, Richard!

Leslie watched me sink into thought, turned back to her computer.

He wants to know what I know. Explaining's easy, but beyond the detail there's no emotion, there's not a whole lot to feel. I doubt he can change that, but there's nothing wrong with me teaching and him learning. Nothing says it has to be a two-way street.

She didn't take her eyes from the computer screen. "Where is he now?"

"We'll see." I closed my eyes. Nothing. No pictures, no child I used to be. Featureless empty black.

"Wookie, does this sound crazy?" I said. "He's gone!"

Twelve

When I threw myself on the bed that night and closed my eyes, the first place I looked was the dungeon cell–block.

"Dickie," I called. "I'm sorry! I forgot!"

The massive door hung open. "Dickie? Hello!"

Inside, nothing. A bench, a cot, the cold flamethrower. He spent decades here because I decided never to be a pawn of feelings, dragged fro and yon decisionless while reason languished. Why did I so exaggerate that choice? Why the overkill—was I not too sure who I was?

There's no question today, I thought, and today I can go back and soften the overkill. So I'm a little late finding my human side. A little late's better than tied to emotional boulders tumbling downhill.

"DICKIE!"

Echoes.

He's somewhere in my mind, I thought. Lots of dark places to hide, if he doesn't want to come out. Why wouldn't he want to be with me? Because he somehow stayed alive on his own all those years and he knows it's not too smart to trust the jailer?

He slipped away when I stopped talking with him, on the way home from the airport. When I changed him from human being to queer mind-trick he was out the door and I didn't even notice.

What's this I've fallen into, I grumbled, do I have to talk to the kid every minute or he runs away?

Maybe not have to talk to him, I thought, but at least clear the brainpath between us of spikes and cobwebs. Maybe care about him would be enough.

"DICKIE!"

No answer.

I lifted in my dream to helicopter altitude, fanned out a search pattern, looking. Rugged hillsides I saw, backrock Arizona, noon sun for heat.

I came back to ground at the edge of a vast dry lake, surface like shattered tiles as far as the eye could see.

Way far out in the middle of that oven stood a small figure.

The distance was farther than it looked, and as I ran to him I wondered why the wicked landscape. Did he choose it or did I?

"DICKIE!"

He turned toward me, watched my advance, but he neither moved nor spoke.

"Dickie," I panted. "What are you doing here?"

"Are you going to lock me up again?"

"No! Never! How can you think I would, after we flew together? That was the most beautiful flight ever in my life, and it was because you were there, flying with me!"

"You cut me off! Soon as we started home, you just stopped thinking about me! I'm the one's got to make up my mind, and don't think I don't know I can leave! I can leave you and never come back! Then where will you be?"

He said that as though I was supposed to answer, as though it would be a catastrophe if he left, as though I hadn't lived without him most of my life already and gotten along fine.

"I'm sorry. Please don't run away."

"I'm easy to forget," he said.

"Can't I know who you are? Can't we be friends?" I'd survive, I thought. But I'd hate for him to vanish now, the innocent undiscovered, lost in the slash-and-burn of my own interiors.

He didn't answer. This may be a long tough haul, I thought, but he's no fool to run from me. Why should he trust a guy who stuffs him in a dungeon and walks away forever? If anybody here's a fool, it's not the little one.

I sat on the dry clay plates of the lake-bed, looked to the hills in the far distance.

"Where are we?" I said.

He said it sadly. "This is my country."

"Your country? Why this place, Dickie? You could have picked any place in my mind, you could have picked anywhere, you could have picked the perfect spot to be, if you wanted."

"This is the perfect spot," he said. "Look at it."

"It's dead! You pick the biggest dry lake in the southern desert and you call it your country, you call it your perfect spot?"

"It's not a dry lake."

"As far as you can see," I said, "flat as an oven, mud cooked into little broken squares mile after mile? If this isn't Death Valley, what is it?"

He looked away from me, off to the distance. "They aren't broken squares," he said. "Every one's different. They're your memories. This desert is your childhood."

Thirteen

Every word in my mind shattered, I was silent for an answer. He's right, I thought at last, this is his country. Those few times I reached for an old memory, here is where I came: dry, dead, lost, everything that used to be, turned to dust. After a while I had shrugged, happy childhood but a terrible memory, and learned to live without my youth, most of it. Here it lay.

He turned and looked at me his grown-up, after all these years, with him in person.

I found my words again. "Are the memories dead for you, too?"

"Of course not, Richard."

"Why do they look that way?"

"They're buried. Every one. I can pull them out if I want." He smiled, as though he had just dumped a bucket of water over my head and he had a thousand buckets left.

"My whole childhood?"

"Yep," he said. "You abandon me, I abandon you."

I fingered the hard earth beneath me, tugged on the crust of a scorched polygon. The clay might as well have been warped steel plate.

"Is the water tower here? Why do I remember the water tower? What does it mean?"

He laughed, mocked my voice as best he could. " 'It was the biggest thing around, I guess.' "

"Dickie, please, I need to know. I'll trade you the airplane ride for the water tower, how's that?"

"I already have the airplane ride," he said. "You owed me that. And you owe me about ten-hundred thousand more."

Nobody said we had to like each other, I thought, but I didn't know it would come to bottom-line negotiations between us, across an iron table. This was never going to work.

70

"Dickie, you're right. I'm sorry. I owe you ten-hundred thousand airplane rides, and I owe you more. I owe you everything I've learned in the years since we were one, and I'm going to pay you that. I promise. You keep your memories. You don't owe me nothin'. I owe you."

His mouth opened in surprise. "Do you mean that?"

"You can run away all you want. I'll keep coming back and trying to make it right, as long as I live."

Then he did the strangest thing. He walked a few feet away, reached to the dry clay and touched one mosaic square, indistinguishable from the others. At his touch, the piece lifted, an amber glass honeycomb from its desert storecase.

"Here's your water tower," he said, and threw the delicate thing to shatter on the ground in front of me.

Fourteen

No sooner had the memory broken apart, pieces still flying, than the world changed around me, total recall. There were rattlesnakes outside the house, I remembered, scorpions inside, centipedes in the shower. But for a boy on an Arizona ranch, these are hazards one can handle.

Don't step into shoes without first bashing them on the floor to let overnight creatures escape. Don't reach under rocks or woodpiles without checking first to see who might call you intruder, and warn by way of attack.

The desert was a sea of sage and rock. Mountains were islands on the rim of the horizon. Everything else crushed flat, time caught in sandstone.

It wasn't so much a water tower, I saw, as it was a windmill. The single vertical dimension in my life was that looming structure. Every day someone's chore to climb the mill's wooden ladder, call out the water-level in the open tank perched high above the rooftop. My brothers managed this as a boring duty. For me, the towering ladder was a hangman's scaffold. It wasn't the height that was terrifying, it was the fall from that height, and I couldn't explain.

Bobby tried to make me climb. "It's your turn, Dickie. Go read the water."

"It's not my turn."

"It's never your turn! Roy climbs up there, I climb up there. You've got to do it, too."

"I'm too little, Bobby, just let me don't do it."

"You're scared, aren't you?" he teased. "Is the little baby scared to climb the tower?"

I wouldn't know for half a century how much I loved my brother, and at times like that it was easy to wish he were dead. "It's too high."

"Little baby's scared to climb," and up he went, not a care, climbed the ladder to the edge of the tank, called 525 gallons, climbed back down, went to our room to read his book.

How easy it would have been for me to admit: you're

right, Bob, I'm just a little baby too scared to climb, I'm a little baby who's pretty damn sure I'm going to slip and fall, crash probably three or four times into the ladder on the way down, shedding limbs as I go, then strike inverted on a sharp rock and I'd just as soon pass that experience by till I'm older, thank you.

Today I can say that and I sense my brother might accept me anyway. At the time, however, admitting babyhood was unthinkable even for babies, and the tower loomed a giant exclamation point after the word *coward*.

I hated that high place as a pin hates the magnet. The tall rough wood was a monument of contempt toward babies, toward sissies controlled by fear, toward boys turned failures before they finished second grade.

From time to time during the year we lived on the ranch, I would find myself alone on the wide first rung of the ladder, twelve inches off the ground. The second rung was a little narrower than the first, and it was twenty-four inches in the air. The third was where it began to get scary, three feet up, and there's where I most often started down.

Dare stand on the fourth, looking up, and the ladder was a wooden railroad track arrowing all but straight up into the sky. The ladder did tilt inward, bolted as it was to the narrow derrick of the water tower, but there was no guardrail, and one's grip on the two-by-four rungs grew weaker with fear the higher one climbed.

I froze at the fifth rung, twenty rungs short of the top of the ladder. Nobody watching, I could fall and kill myself from here. What if they were watching, what difference would that make, Dickie? You can still kill yourself. You are on your own, and it is time to come down. One thing about sitting on the ground: you are completely safe from falling.

Carefully, so carefully, I eased one foot down and then the other, down to the sand. Back to earth, I trembled in relief and rage.

I *hate* being a coward! I am terrified of dying. Why must I risk my life over something that is just plain standing here and doesn't care what I do and nobody asks me anymore to climb the stupid tower anyway?

I leaned against the wood. It wasn't so bad on the third rung. I can climb to the third rung and get used to it, and come down if I want or go up if I want. If I can climb to the third rung and whistle, I'm okay. If I can't whistle, I'll stay till I can whistle or I'll come down and nobody will know.

Cursing towers is not easy when one doesn't know any curse-words beyond *darn,* and *darn* was to be my limit for many years to come. *Darn* does not convert fear into anger the way a modern vocabulary does—it was a long slow climb all the way to rung five.

But the idea worked. Make friends with each rung, step by step. Each has a personality . . . if I stay long enough to talk with every rung, I might be able to climb.

When I could whistle at five, I stepped to six. Long time there . . . hard to breathe, harder to whistle. Why does this feel so high, I'm only six feet off the ground . . .

. . . my *feet* are only six feet off the ground. My head, the center of consciousness and life and being, is nearly ten feet up! No air for a whistle.

But hey! If that's so, I don't have to climb nineteen more rungs! I only have to climb enough so I can see over the top of the tank—my feet don't have to look in the tank, just my eyes . . . that's three and a half rungs that I don't have to climb!

I whistled at six, went up to seven.

Don't look down, my brothers had told me.

A weak whistle, and I felt as comfortable as I did watching a scorpion crawl toward me on the bed. Rather be here on this ladder than have a scorpion crawling toward me, stinger up over its head, claws open. Whistle. Another step.

I felt my hands loosening on the rungs, threw my right arm over the two-by-four and locked it to my chest. The arm will have to come off before I fall.

Or the whole step might pull loose and I'll go over backward. What am I doing here? I am going to get killed for no reason at all! *Why am I doing this?*

I was at rung seventeen, clinging with both arms around the wood, by now less than two feet wide. At my shoulder was the dark-shingle side of the water tank, comforting mass but nothing to hang on to, nothing to grab when the steps break away from the tower. No whistle. It was all I could do to hug wood and keep from screaming terror, and there were three rungs yet to climb.

Two rungs, I told myself. Only two more steps. I don't care if there are three to go, there are only two to go. I will not look down down down. I will look up. *I will lift mine eyes unto the hills* . . . Dad prays at the dinner table, where nobody's going to fall off the side. Holy *cow* this is high! Two more rungs.

Two rungs higher, I went sick at the sight of the rim of the tank. Not at the sight, but at the thought that the rim was close enough to grab with both hands and if I did I would be hanging from the edge and there would be no way I could kick my way back onto the ladder again and I'd just hang there in space until my fingers slowly let go . . .

Why am I thinking like this? What's happened to my mind? Stop stop stop. Think about one more rung.

There's tar all over the rim of the tank. Somebody once climbed up here, not only climbed up here, but climbed up here with a pot of tar in one hand and a brush in the other and he painted tar all over the top edge so the wood wouldn't rot! Was he scared? He was here before I ever came and he wasn't terrified he was going to fall, he was worried about wood-rot . . . he must have sat on the edge of the tank, worked his way all around it, painting till he was out of tar and then climbed down, got some more, climbed back up again and finished the job!

What am I so scared of? I don't have to paint anything, I don't have to do anything, I just have to do one more rung and look over the side of this tank tank tank.

It was fifteen inches wide, that last rung I reached for, hauled myself up, looking up to the wheel of the windmill; huge, now, six feet over my head.

See the bolts and rivets on the blades, spots of rust. A faint breeze stirred the blades an inch and when it stopped a second later the wheel turned back that same inch. The sight of the wheel close-up made things if possible worse. The scale was terribly wrong . . . the wheel ought to be small, the highest object for miles. Please it shouldn't be this massive disk just above my head, because that meant that *I* was almost the highest object, with the farthest to fall of anything in sight.

What if somebody saw me now? Please no, somebody

would call to me and if I had to answer and hold on at the same time I couldn't do it and I'd fall. Please Bobby please Roy, please do not come out and see me.

I turned my head, inch by agonizing inch, looked over the edge of the tank. Down the inside, neat white numbers painted, low numbers at the bottom, high numbers at the top. And in the bottom of the tank, so strange this way high in the air: water! Greenclear water, not very deep, a still pool just below the number 400.

Roy has stood here, and seen that number, Bobby has stood here on this very spot where I am this minute. I know I'll die in a few seconds when an earthquake shakes me loose or the wind blows me off, but *I am as brave as my brothers!*

All I have to go is down, one step at a time, but already right now I have WON! I have already WON!

I forced a rigid death-grin, sticking like a starved leech to the sky. They will NEVER call me scared again!

Ever so slowly, I turned my head, looked away from the tank, away from the tower.

While I climbed, someone had changed the world. Way below, our rooftop, soot in the chimney, shingles missing here and there, a marvelous detailed toy house for toy people no bigger than my finger. Cactus not monster sentinels but harmless pincushion dwarfs. There the burros grazing in the corral, soft as squirrels, there the gate, and even there the highway, Bisbee one way, Phoenix a hundred miles gone the other. *If I could fly!*

There the mountains, for all my height, still above me. Some day, Dickie, they whispered. When you look down on us, will you think the world's a toy? And how will you play if it is?

I shivered, ice terror for every smallest move of eyes or neck, trembling without control. I'll fall and die before ever I make it safe to the ground, but I've never seen . . .

From the air . . . everything changes! *It's beautiful!* How can life be so plain on the ground and such glory from the air?

Fifteen

*D*ickie looked down at me where I sat on the lake-bed, the smallest trace of relief in his face. One memory lifted, from the weight of thousands.

"When?" I asked, dazed with what he had shown me.

"We were seven. You turned into a grown-up and went off on your own when I was nine, when Bobby died. After that, only the future mattered to you, you wanted to grow up and get out and you wanted to travel light." He wasn't complaining, he was reminding me what I knew.

"You left me all the memories you didn't want. Here they are, every one, but they teach me nothing, I can't read them without you." His voice faded, so faint I could barely hear over the silence of the desert. "You could show me what they mean."

He looked at me in silence, lashed still by the mysteries that had driven me relentless through childhood. Am I the only one can step between him and his ignorance, I thought, the only one can grab the whip from its hand, am I the only rescuer he'll ever know?

"Tell me!" he said. "I need to know! I remember everything, and nothing means anything!"

Instead of melting in his pain, I frowned. "Of course it doesn't, Dickie. Nothing means anything."

"But they're not empty memories for you!" He was desperate to climb what was for him a glass wall, oiled in question marks. "The water tower! Richard, you know what it means!"

I reached up from where I sat, to touch his shoulder. "I know what it means for me, Dickie. But the water tower has a million other meanings that I didn't choose, meanings that aren't true for me. Nothing has meaning until it changes what we think and who we are."

"You're talking like a grown-up," he said. "Nothing has meaning?"

"Until you process; what happened; in your mind," I

said. "Climbing the water tower means zero until you give it meaning. Decide that your lesson, clinging way up in the air, is that altitude equals terror, and your whole life changes. 'A future with heights? Not for me! Never altitude, please, thank you!'

"That decision," I said, "that lesson you invented, makes ten thousand futures more likely for you, erases ten thousand others, including by the way mine. No heights means no airplanes means no flight means no paragliding means no Shepherd means no remembering Dickie means no opening his cell means no you and me in the middle of this lake of memories."

"You didn't decide that altitude equals terror."

"Too beautiful, Dickie! From the top of that windmill, terror was in lowercase, WONDER! was in caps. The meaning I picked, the one that changed my life: *Overcome fear, behold wonder.* It's still true."

I watched his eyes. "You're the only person who can decide if my truth is true for you or if it's nonsense," I said. "The principles I'd die for, the highest rights I know—for you they're suggestions, they're possibilities. You choose, you live the consequences. Every *yes, no, maybe,* creates the school you call your personal experience."

I thought the weight would pause him a bit, but in a second he leaned toward me, a racer at the gate. "In fifty years, you've decided, for yourself of course, what everything means, *how everything works*?"

"As a matter of fact," I said modestly, "most of it, I have."

Sixteen

S ince lunatic Shepherd told me about a book for the boy I had been, one level of my mind had been, busily at work, laying it out for him.

"Say it simply," said Dickie. Was that dread in his voice, his dream to know come true but too complicated to follow?

I had tried this before, saying what I think about the world, without much success. It does take a little theory, after all, a little development to lay foundations. But every time, invariably, two or three hours into basics, my listeners topple like stone idols, eyes open but gazing blank into space. Just when I get to the interesting part they're wheeled away unhearing.

With Dickie, at last, it would be different. Nothing I

find so electrifying would be hard for me to understand at any age.

"To find your way on earth," I said, settling myself on the desert floor, "you need to understand two things: the power of consent and the purpose of happiness. But before you can know those, you need to know the principle of the universe itself. Simple. Two words: *Life Is*. Everything else follows in what I call a logical cascade. Here's the way . . ."

He was kneeling on the ground, his eyes nearly level with mine. "What's it like to be old?"

"Excuse me?" Was this bright child not following me?

"What does it feel like," he said, "to be old?"

I blinked at him. "What about the way the universe works?"

"You're making it up," he said. "I want to know what you know."

"*Making it up?* This is my life we're talking about, this is everything you said you wanted to learn! I think it's darned important, the principle of the universe. I would have given anything to find out, when I was you. Besides, the one thing I don't know about is age. I don't believe in age."

"You can't not believe in it!" he said. "How old are you?"

"I stopped counting, way long ago. Too dangerous."

"Dangerous?" He may not have been interested in my home-built philosophy, but age was important. How we change!

"Counting is dangerous," I said. "When you're a kid, getting older is fun. It's parties and presents and Birthday Boy and chocolate cake. But careful, Dickie. Every year in that cake is a hook, and if you swallow too many hooks you're caught on an idea you can't shake loose later on."

"Really?" He thought I was kidding.

"How do children die?" I said.

"They fall out of trees," he said, "they get run over by trolley-cars, they get buried in caves . . ."

"Exactly," I said. "What's your last name?"

He wrinkled his forehead, cocked his head at me. Has the old guy forgotten? "Bach."

"Wrong," I said. "That's your second-to-last name. Your real last name, in this culture, is a number, and the number is your age. You aren't Dickie Bach, you are . . ."

". . . Dickie Bach, Nine."

"Hey for you!" I said. "And people with low-number last names almost always die from Unlucky Bad Things—they're in the wrong place at the wrong time. Jimmy Merkle, Six, held on to a too-big bunch of balloons, the wind blew him out to sea and he never came back. Annie Fisher, Fourteen, was trapped undersea in a sunken side-wheeler when it rolled off the continental shelf. Dickie Bach, Twelve, blew himself up making hydrazine rocket fuel with his chemistry set."

He nodded, lines out to fathom where I was going.

"But people with high-number last names," I said, "die from Inevitable Bad Things; there's no escape. Mr. James Merkle, Eighty-four, lost his battle last week with terminal lethargy. Ms. Anne Fisher-Stovall, Ninety-seven, overwhelmed by Lothman's Disease. Mr. Richard Bach, One-hundred forty-five, died of hopeless old age."

He laughed at the last, age 145 is impossible. "Okay," he said. "So what? What's wrong with birthdays?"

"When the numbers are little, you know you don't have to die. When the numbers are big . . ."

". . . you do."

"*High last number, I have to die*. It's called a default belief, when you agree to rules before you think, when you go along because you're expected to. Thousands of those in a lifetime, unless you're careful."

"And default beliefs are bad," he said.

"Not all of them. If we don't accept any common beliefs, we can't exist in spacetime. But when we don't believe in age, at least we don't have to die because our numbers change."

"I like the cake," he said.

"One candle for every year. Do you eat the candles?"

He made a face. "No!"

"Cake any day you want. Just don't eat cake with candles."

"I like presents."

"Give up birthdays, you can get your own presents, every day of the year."

He was quiet for a minute, considering that. Everybody he knew had a birthday. "Are you demented?" he asked.

I threw back my head and laughed, remembering. Always at home our values were cerebral. The first grown-up word I learned was *vocabulary*. Mom taught me to read at home, before first grade, and I felt oh-so-smart because my parents valued intelligence instead of feeling. Emotions we controlled, intellect ran wild.

Not only could I use *demented,* I remembered, I knew *fiduciary, egregious* and *polysyllabic.* For show there was *antidisestablishmentarianism* and *diisobutylphenoxypolyethoxyethanol.* Never much cared for the first of my show words, but to this day I love the roll and lilt of the second, and use it as often as I can.

"Of course I'm demented, Dickie. In a nice way."

"You just took away my birthdays. Is that the kind of nice you mean?"

"Yes. The nice that is freedom from convention. I took something else away, too."

"What?"

"When you don't believe in birthdays, the idea of aging turns a little foreign to you. You don't fall into trauma over your sixteenth birthday or your thirtieth or the big Five-Oh or the deadly Century. You measure your life by what you learn, not by counting how many calendars you've seen. If you're going to have trauma, better it be the shock of discovering the fundamental principle of the universe than some date predictable as next July."

"The other kids will point at me—The Boy with No Birthday."

"They will. You decide. If you think there's one good reason to count how many times you've ridden this planet around its sun, keep your birthdays, count your little clock. Swallow a hook every year and pay the price like everybody else."

"You're manipulating me," he said.

"I'd be manipulating you if I forced you to give up birthdays when you really want to count them. If you haven't given them up, I haven't manipulated you."

He looked at me sideways, to warn that he wasn't kidding. "Are you really an adult?"

"Try it on yourself," I said. "Are you really a child?"

"I'm supposed to be, but I feel so much older! Do you feel like a grown-up?"

"Never," I said.

"So the funny feeling stays? When I'm young I feel old, and when I'm old I feel young?"

"According to me," I said, "we're ageless creatures. The funny feeling that we're younger or older than our body is the contrast between common sense—our consciousness *ought* to feel as old as our body—and the truth, that consciousness has no age at all. Our minds just can't put that together by any rules of spacetime, so instead of trying other rules it just quits trying. Whenever we sense we're not the same age as our numbers, we say *weird feeling!* and change the subject."

"What if we don't change the subject? What's the answer?"

"Don't label age. Don't say, 'I'm seven,' or 'I'm ninety.' As soon as you tell yourself 'I'm ageless!' there's nothing to contrast, and the weird feeling's gone. Really. Try it."

He closed his eyes. "I'm ageless," he whispered, and in a moment he smiled. "Interesting."

"True?"

"It works," he said.

"If our body is a perfect expression of our thought about body," I said, "and if our thought about body is that its condition has everything to do with inner image and nothing to do with time, then we don't have to be impatient for being too young or frightened of being too old."

"Who says body is a perfect expression of thought? Where did that come from?"

I slapped my hand to my forehead. "Ah! That's philosophy! I'm just making it up, didn't you say, too hard and boring for somebody who's only nine?"

He looked at me evenly, hint of a smile. "Who's nine?"

Seventeen

"*D*ickie, let me tell you a story."

"I like stories," he said.

"This story is from my memory, not yours. You remember my past, I remember your future. One of them, anyway. But instead of telling, I'll show you, all right?"

"All right," he said cautiously, more curious now than frightened. "Is this more philosophy?"

"A story. A true story from your yet-to-be. Hold on to my mind, watch what happens. Then tell me if it's philosophy or not."

Ever so slowly, Dickie was becoming a friend, game for adventure. "Ready, go!"

I closed my eyes and remembered.

There was a massive long steel beam, hanging heavy and level from a single silver cable, high over my inner empty space. Years I had lived, learned, played on that beam, stayed so close to the center that it rarely tilted, and then barely enough to notice.

But in adolescence all values are tested.

"I know what let's do," Mike said. It was summertime, midday in his house, his father at work, his mother gone shopping. Mike and Jack and I were all three bored. In secret, I'd idly considered that it wouldn't be the end of the world for school to start again, before too long.

"What let's do?" I said.

"Let's have a drink!"

At once I was nervous. He did not mean lemonade. "Drink what?"

"Drink BEER!"

"Hey, you're talkin'!" said Jack. "You got some BEER?"

"Ton of it. Let's set 'em up!"

I was being pushed where I didn't want to go . . . all at once thrown farther from my center than I had ever

95

been, and the beam that meant balance in my life tilted ponderously beneath me.

"I'm not sure this is smart," I said. "Your dad's gonna find out. When he comes home and the beer's gone . . ."

"Nah," said Mike. "He's got too much, they're having a party tonight. He'll never notice a little bit's gone."

Mike disappeared into the kitchen and returned, three bottles by their scrawny necks in one hand, three glasses in the other, bottle opener in his teeth. He set the glasses on the coffee table.

This is crazy, I thought. I'm not old enough to drink!

"Will he kill you when he finds out," I asked, "or just cripple you for life?"

"He won't find out," said my friend. "Come on, we've got to do this sooner or later. Might as well be sooner. Right, Jack?"

"Sure."

"RIGHT, JACKIE?"

"RIGHT!"

"RIGHT, DICK?"

"I don't know. I guess."

"Let's pour 'em out, for two men and a little baby."

"Oh, knock it off," I said.

Who knows, I thought. This is supposed to be delicious stuff. Cold on a hot day. All men drink beer except my dad. One glass is probably not enough to get drunk on, and if it's as good as they say, what does it matter if I'm supposed to be a few years too young?

The steel balance within leaned so wildly it was all I could do to stay on top. I didn't know what would happen if I fell, but I was not interested in finding out.

Mike hissed the tops off the bottles, sloshed foaming yellow stuff to our glass-brims.

He lifted his beer with relish, licking his lips. "Down the hatch, guys. Here's to ya!"

We drank.

Half a swallow and my throat clutched. Cold, yes. Delicious? Awful! This does not feel right. I am way too young to drink beer.

"Gakh!" I said. "This is supposed to be *good*?"

"Good *for* ya!" said Mike, glass high, looking round at us all.

"Yeah," said Jack. "I could get used to that."

"Oh, come on, you guys," I said. "You're crazy! This stuff tastes like my chemistry set, they poured it in a pan and left it to rot!"

"*Ferment*—the word is *ferment*." Mike forgot we were friends. "It's beer, for Cry sake! It's not how it tastes, or you don't like it! You like it after you drink more. But now, *you have to drink it!*"

I froze in fear . . . did I have to do this no matter what feels right to me? Is this growing up, when you have to do what other people do? I don't like what's happening here. How do I get out of this? Help!

For answer there was an explosion in the back of my mind, doors blown off their hinges, a livid force crashing in, seething:

This jerk thinks he's gonna tell you what you do and what you don't do? What does he mean, *you have to*? You don't have to *nothin'* if you don't want to! This clown's trying to tell YOU to do what HE wants?

I slammed the glass down on the table, beer flying out

the top. "I do NOT *have to,* Mike! NOBODY tells me I *have to* ANYTHING!"

The two stared at me wordless, drinks frozen midair.

"I do NOT!" I sprang to my feet, pure rage, daring them to lift a finger to stop me. *"NOBODY!"*

Storming out, slamming the door behind me, I watched as astonished as the two boys. Who is this wildman took me over? That's not just overdoing things a little bit that's somebody I've never seen, lunged from behind grabbed me threw me out of the way didn't care what I thought, what anybody thought he is super darn MAD!

I stalked down the street toward my house, swiftly cooling, noticed all at once that the giant steel balance under me had gone level and steady as deep wide granite. I blinked, smiled a little, laughed out loud, walking fast. That guy is . . . ferocious! And he's me! He's on my side! Who *are* you, guy?

Nobody forces you to do anything. Get that, Dick? Ever! Nobody! Not Mike or Jack or Mom or Dad or *anybody* in your life forces you to do what you do not want to do!

My jaw dropped open. *You care about me!*

Yeah. Other people care about you, too, you won't meet

till later. You matter, kid, and if you're too chicken to defend yourself, I'll do it for you!

Now wait, I thought, Mike's my friend. I don't have to defend myself from my own friends!

Dumb, dumb, dumb. Listen, because you're not going to see me till you're way off balance and scared again. Mike is not your friend. Learn now that the best friend you have is Dick Bach. Lots of levels of yourself, and you can call on us when you want. Nobody knows you, nobody really knows you, but us. You can destroy yourself or you can fly beyond the stars, and *nobody cares, nobody stays with you through it all but us!*

After a minute I thought thanks for saving me, back there. Sorry I'm dumb. There's a lot to learn.

No answer.

I said thank you, do you hear? I mean it!

No answer. My tough inner bodyguard was gone.

Eighteen

"That's going to happen to me?" asked Dickie, dazzled by the future, a little scared.

"If you make the choices I did, it will. But something happened, a consequence to that minute, you ought to know."

"Show me," he said.

✦

Slowing my walk, short of home, I turned aside to a vacant lot, wild wheat tall and green, and sank down into grass softening the contour of a hideaway I had dug the summer before.

I lay on my back, looked up to the sky, watched summer clouds float high overhead, shapes framed in mint, gliding on the breeze.

Any voice in my mind, I had always thought, had to be my own wordless talk, echoes in an empty cavern. Sometimes thoughtful, sometimes chattering fragments to which I barely listened, spirit jogging words to keep out the cold.

But different levels inside? Parts of me I hadn't met? I bubbled with curiosity.

If the inner voices are more than echoes, are they family I can train from random chatter to become teachers and guides?

I frowned. No. There's no training someone to be my own teacher. How would I do such a thing?

It felt like research at a giant microscope. The answer was under the lens, but just out of focus. I was right on the edge, just a tiny little turn, here, careful . . .

What if my teachers are here, right now?

Instead of always talking, in my mind, what if for a change I *listen*?

Never had the world been so sharp, never colors so clear. Grass and sky and clouds, even the wind was bright.

My teachers already exist!

What if all these levels inside of me are my *friends,* and they know a lot more than I know? It would be as if . . .

". . . as if you were captain of a sailing frigate, sir, a very young captain of a wonderful fast ship."

At once in my mind the sky and clouds flashed to a different scene: there a boy in blue uniform, gold epaulets, standing aslant on the quarterdeck of an ebony-hull fighting boat, sleek clouds of canvas angling aloft.

Did I invent the scene, or did someone paint this picture in lightning?

The ship drove along, lee scuppers awash, slicing deep swells asunder: boy on deck, uniformed crew working near.

Fascinated, I jumped the play forward in my mind, too fast. Shoals ahead, monster coral knives underwater.

"Breakers!" a lookout cried. "Dead ahead!"

The ship urged unswerving on, every timber and line and yard of canvas, every life on board driving straight through, course unchanged.

"The breakers are reefs, aren't they?" I asked, for in a blink I had understood, and become the boy. "If we don't change course, we'll hit the reefs, won't we?"

The first mate's sunleather face impassive, a voice from years already under sail. "Aye, sir, we will."

"Tell them to turn!"

"You may take the wheel yourself, Captain, or you may order the helmsman," said the mate. "He'll obey no command but yours."

I could see from the quarterdeck, blue water exploding to foam a dozen ship-lengths ahead.

No one commands this vessel but the captain.

I turned to the helm, more frightened than commanding. "Hard about!"

Wheel-spokes blurred instantly underhand, the ship slewed, curtains of spray flying, a mustang spun full gallop at sea.

Aloft, crew sprang to sheets and braces as the frigate careened upwind, slammed from port tack to starboard, canvas booming thunder in the sky.

On the quarterdeck, officers watched, hanging on, not a word to the captain. The master's age doesn't matter, nor does the consequence of his order. The crew's duty is to execute the master's command. Comment is made only at such time as the captain shall request.

The picture was brighter than full-color theater, and it was my life onscreen.

I didn't invent the picture. I asked for it, but I didn't invent it. Is there an invisible crew about me? Who handed me that image?

"Here, sir."

Was the voice imagined too, clear as the picture?

"Aye, sir. We speak a language you've put aside for a while. It's your imagination translates our knowing into pictures and words that serve you on your voyage."

"And you speak only when spoken to?"

"In words, yes. Otherwise we're feelings, intuition, conscience."

The frigate hissed ahead, as eager to turn this direction as that, any way I wished. I walked aft, grasped a mizzen shroud with both hands. My ship! Why should an idea that felt so right be so hard to believe?

"I'm in command," I said, a last confirmation.

"Aye, sir."

"And you're the one who saved me, from Mike and the beer?"

"No, sir. That was . . . in this picture, he's the second mate. We'd give our lives for you, sir, but in different ways, and the Second thinks more in blacks and whites than the rest of us. When he sees you in danger, he pretty well comes out swinging, sir."

"The rest of you don't?"

"We're each of us different."

My whole life I'd felt alone. I'd been a quiet kid with a vague *something,* something powerful and good, fashioned about me that I couldn't understand.

All at once I knew. The something was my ship, and her secret crew. Never had I understood that I *command,* with absolute authority, the ship of my life! I decide its mission and rules and discipline, at my word waits every tool and sail, every cannon, the strength of every soul on board. I'm master of a team of passionate skills to sail me through hell's own jaws the second I nod the direction to steer.

"Why didn't you tell me you exist?" I said. "There's so much I have to learn! I need you! Why didn't you tell me you were with me?"

I lay in the grass and listened to the wind.

"We didn't tell, sir," came the answer, "because you didn't ask."

✦

I opened my eyes into a long silence, Dickie sitting near, eyes closed, studying the ship.

"What do you think?" I asked. "Philosophy or not, little guy?"

He opened his eyes. "I don't know," he said, watching me. "But from now on, call me *Captain*."

I touched him with my fist, soft enough to say *that's not a bad idea*.

Nineteen

*I*t's beyond my curiosity, I thought, staring in the mirror without seeing, patting macho-brand perfume to my face. Medicine is a wrong-way street.

I'm numbed by medicine's sanctimony, appalled by its tenets. A drug for everything is madness. Legal or not, prescribed or not, over-counter under-counter bought for blood on street-corners—every pill separates us from knowing our own completion and from being taught by what's true. We're better treated by choosing no drugs whatever, at all, for any purpose. It's criminal, I thought, for me to support a crowd that treats body as machine instead of thought manifest, that fails to see beyond the first screen of appearance.

Leslie's my opposite. Medical books on her lap in bed, she reads for hours, eyes like saucers. Frowning sometimes, muttering, "Nutrition! Exercise! How can they ignore them?" but delighting withal in the complexity of medical consequence.

She can read whatever she wants, I reminded myself, she can study frog-and-chicken spells if she likes. But *moi*? Support a system of pill-bent whitecoats too distracted to see we're begging our own attention with a spectrum of creative ills? Not likely!

In this mind I found myself dressing for the hospital charity ball.

A privilege, Leslie had thought, an invitation for us to help in the smallest way the advancement of knowledge over killer disease and painful dying.

"Let's go!" I had said. I rarely see my wife dressed to dance. Demolishing my principles, supporting research to drag consciousness backward, what a small price for the sight!

I shrugged into my darkest jacket, pushed a little Cessna airplane-pin into the lapel, polished it with my thumb.

"Help me with this, will you, sweetie?" she called from the bathroom. "The waist is fine, but either this top has shrunk or my top is getting bigger."

I'm always glad to lend a hand, and rushed to help my wife.

"There! Thank you!" she said, first glance into the mirror. She adjusted a sleeve. "What do you think? Does it work?"

She heard the thud behind her, turned after a minute to help me stand again, leaned me against the doorjamb and waited for a spoken critique.

The dress was soft liquid black, the top slit down in front as far as the skirt slit up the side, spiraling her body in a long sensual embrace.

"Nice," I gasped, diagonally. "Very nice."

I tottered to the counter, pressed a brush against my hair. Any attempt, I thought, however desperate, to look as if I belonged with this woman when we stepped into the ballroom.

She studied the mirror, measuring her image by a hundred harsh standards, coming away doubtful. "It's not too spicy, is it?"

My voice broke. "As long as you don't leave the bedroom," I managed, "it's fine."

She frowned at me in the mirror. When Leslie dresses formal, her values revert to her uncompromising Hollywood past, and that's serious business. "Come on, Richie!

110

Tell me what you really think. If it's too much, I'll take it off . . ."

Take it off, I thought. Let's stay home tonight, Leslie, let's just slip into the other room, let's bit by bit ever so slowly take off your deep-shadow Oscar-night dress, and forget about going anywhere for the next week or so.

"No," I told her, to my disgust at chances lost. "It's a dear little outfit. A fitting gown, an extremely well-fitting I might add gown for the ball. Full moon tonight, police probably won't even answer the phone."

She stayed skeptical. "I got this just before we met, Richie, it's twenty years old," she said. "Would the white silk be better?"

"Probably better," I told her in the mirror. "Safer, for sure. Nobody in this town has ever in their lives seen a dress like this one." Twenty years, and even for courtesy I couldn't keep from staring. She's enchanted me, I thought. Leslie can always dress to kill when she wants to, but honest, this is going to be mass murder!

I remembered a note I had written before we met, found years later at the bottom of a file: "Lovers growing into each other's ideals, they each turn more attractive with time." Now it was true, there she stood adjusting her necklace just so, was it better one strand or two? The woman in the mirror was my wife!

I stared and wondered. Does she look so grand because there's a subjective bell jar over lovers . . . no matter how they change to the world, they're beautiful to each other? Or is it deliberate, has it happened because we make it important, our gift to each other to look better every year?

No smoking, no drinking, no drugs, no other intimate men or women. No meat, no coffee, no sugar, no fat, no chocolate, no overwork, no stress. Slow down, less food, tough workouts, gardening and paragliding, swimming and yoga and air and fresh juice, music and study and talk and sleep. Each its own fierce struggle to give up or to make time for against an avalanche of objections, each a deliberate goal, won after a few or many distressing backslides. Chocolate my worst demon, merciless workdays hers.

"You can't give up that much without some reward," I said.

"Pardon?" It was nearly time to leave. A lock of blond hair wanted to curl left, she was patiently putting it right. Too late to change clothes. The killer gown would be going with us. How do they make women's clothes cling to such impossible curves?

"I can hardly breathe, you're so beautiful."

She turned away from the glass and smiled at me. "You mean it, don't you?" She held out her arms. "Oh, Wookie, thank you. I'm sorry I get so concentrated, sometimes. I don't want you to be ashamed of me when we go out."

I hugged her and turned her loose to finish. Why is appearance so important? Used to be, I thought beauty was an unworthy condition to require of a mate. I required it, but didn't know why . . . isn't it what lies within that matters?

I must have known what before why, back then. Had my wife and I not been beautiful to each other, we never would have made it through storms when all else was lost. "I don't understand her," I gnashed, more than once. "Stubborn crazy perfectionist! If she weren't so damn beautiful, I swear I'd leave forever!"

And yet there were beautiful women in my past whom I left without a second thought, when we had learned all we had come to learn from each other. Some striking women, you get to know them, they turn plain. Unique others, soulmates, the better friends you are, the more beautiful they become.

Were Leslie and I like that? Could I have guessed that jack-o'-light Beauty might curl up with us to stay, then glow more brightly yet? Never happened to me but once, and here she stands.

She finished abruptly with the mirror, whirled a black

silk stole around her shoulders, reached for her purse. "I'm on time!"

"Good!"

"Do you love me?"

"Yes," I said.

"I don't know why . . ."

"Because you are loving, warm, witty, resourceful, kind, inquisitive, sensual, intelligent, creative, calm, many-faceted, free, open, outgoing, responsive, scintillating, practical, delightful, beautiful, positive, talented, articulate, orderly, insightful, mysterious, protean, curious, lighthearted, unpredictable, powerful, determined, adventurous, earnest, sincere, unafraid and wise."

"Gee!" she said. "I'll be on time more often!"

Twenty

I felt like Robin Hood disguised, when we entered, and the ballroom twin to the one in Nottingham. People nodded and laughed and glittered, sipped bubbles from long-stem crystal. Trapped, I thought; me the militant drugophobe, surrounded by physicians of every call. I'm doomed at the first Aspirin Toast, they'll catch me dumping mine in the potted palm, there'll go up a cry and hue, a roar of fingers pointed.

The staircase, I thought. I'll dash up the staircase, leap to the drapes, swing through those tall French doors, exploding glass and splinters, vault over the balcony to the ledge, scramble up gargoyle walls to the rooftops and away into the night.

I'm a self-taught dropout, a hay-stem aviator salesperson of biplane rides late from Midwest pastures, a bankrupt barely recovered from the lowest fiscal caste . . . what could I possibly have in common with these sophisticates? Why earn my way into the world's tiniest minority, All Drugs Are Evil, then rush out to the Majority Ball? To watch my wife, I remembered.

Leslie's eyes sparkled as I lifted the silken stole from her shoulders.

I took her hand, paused a beat or two on the edge of the hardwood floor, then let wood dissolve to plains of wheat, and she and I the grand and graceful, we the sweeping airs curved in from Austria, drawn by gallant Strauss isobars. There's no telling what we look like, dancing, but that's the way it feels, aloft with the music.

"You'd think doctors would get enough of anatomy, day after day," I told her as we turned.

"Yes?" she said regally. Her hair moved in the wind of the dance.

"No. Since you walked in, I haven't yet seen the back of a man's head."

"Silly," she said, though what I said was mostly true.

How safe it was, before I learned to dance! To be master of the dance vicarious takes neither risk nor effort, and that's the kind of master that's easiest for me to be.

Vicariosity, however, lacks the exhilaration of music flooding body in motion. To gain that, I had to find my way to a real floor and learn real dancing, with my body, stumbling fool-like in some mirrored lesson-hall. Grim thought. I haven't traveled this far, I had told my wife, to become a clumsy beginner again, in anything.

Leslie didn't agree, and took lessons without me, coming home so radiant from her dance-nights that I wondered. What could be so much fun about dancing?

She showed me a step or two, and in a moment dignified safety became less interesting than learning with her.

So, sure enough, my fears came true. For weeks I was the creature escaped from Frankenstein's basement, and worse. Electrodes through the brain would have been less glaring than my monster boots crushing all but the most nimble instructor underfoot. Don't quit, though, and sooner or later . . .

Now I gave myself up to the music, saw no one in the ballroom but her. Thank you, brave earlier Richard, I thought, for running at last from your wallflower safety! It felt like heaven in the music, and my wife must have been thinking the same.

"When you were a little boy, Wookie, did you think sometimes you came to earth from way out in the stars?"

"M-hm. I knew it." My homemade telescopes, I remembered. Looking through eyepieces was like looking through spaceship windows, searching for home.

"I knew it, too," she said. "Not from a planet that even exists. Just from Out There."

I nodded, eased us around other dancers, reverse left spirals into reverse right. "If anybody asked me to point the way home," I said, "I would have pointed up, and I didn't know why till not so long ago."

She cocked her head.

"I couldn't point inside: a tight space cluttered with body parts, barely room to breathe. Couldn't point left or right: those directions took me nowhere but a different here. The only way left to point was up, away from earth, so for a long time I was homesick for the stars."

"I still am," she said. "If the saucer-people come down and land on the roof, wouldn't we say 'take us home'?"

The picture made me smile. Our roof isn't strong enough to land a spaceship. Would we fly with visitors from outer space after they had squashed our kitchen flat?

"They couldn't take us home," I said. "The stars aren't where we came from. How can people from beyond space-time point the way home?"

"There have to be maps," she said.

I couldn't answer, thought about what she said till the music found its way back to its beginnings, sighed and stopped at last.

There are maps, I thought. I wasn't pointing to the stars, back then, I was pointing away from earth. When I knew inside that home isn't a planet, I was trying to show me home isn't *any* "where," but I didn't get the message till not so long ago.

We found our way to a table, met strangers: a doctor and his wife, a hospital administrator and her husband. What do I say after How do you do? I wondered.

Do you feel in any way responsible for the drug-based society seething around us? Does it make you happy to believe we're helpless passengers in our bodies? Is it true that more than any professional group it is doctors who fear death, that their suicide rate is higher than any other?

Any umbrologists here? I thought of asking.

Umbrologists?

A physician who treats disorders of the shadow, I would have said: broken shadows, deformed shadows, missing shadows, hyperumbria—abnormal activity of the shadow. You know, *umbrologist*! Any umbrologists here?

That's insane, they would have laughed. Whatever body does, shadow imitates.

Likewise is it insane, I would have said, to forget that whatever belief does, body imitates? No umbrologist here? Just every doctor in the room. And then I would have walked away.

I didn't say any such thing, and I walked nowhere.

"You fly a Skymaster!" the administrator said.

I looked at her. Do physicians read minds?

"The pin in your lapel," she said. "That's a Cessna Skymaster, isn't it?"

"Oh! Of course. Yes it is," I said. "Not many people notice."

"I fly a Cessna 210," she said. "Same as a Skymaster, almost. Single-engine Skymaster."

"Cessna, Cessna, Cessna," said the other doctor. "Am I the only one at the table who flies a Piper product? How either of you can pass up a Twin Comanche, I can't guess."

"Full throttle and a little dive," I said, "it's not so hard to do." To my surprise, I was smiling.

After a minute I looked at Leslie and she shrugged an innocent what do you know . . . a night of dance and airplanes can't be all bad.

And so the evening sailed past. We danced often. I remembered that many physicians are also aviators, the hall was crowded with doctor-pilots. By midnight we had met and liked a dozen of them, and impossibly, I felt at home.

So they have a different point of view, I thought, that's not the end of the world. They're doing the best they know, they're not enslaving people into medicine against their will, there's room for all of us in the sky.

There was no Aspirin Toast, I wasn't forced to escape to the rooftops in a shower of French glass. That was a nine-year-old's fantasy, I thought, Dickie watching tense, fight-or-flight from behind curtains in my eyes.

Leslie's killer dress was delight in motion, gentlemen appreciating without riot, ladies, unintimidated, swirling in their own bright elegance.

✦

"I learned so much tonight!" said my wife on our way home.

"Are they numbered?"

She smiled. "One: Us Dancing! We're not the two we used to be. We're better, and I like it!"

"Me, too."

"Two: You, Too. You liked getting dressed up and going to a ball! With people who believe in medicine! I didn't let on, but I half expected you'd wind up at swordpoint tonight, outnumbered and surrounded and fighting to death that body is mind so why treat it with chemicals when a change of thought et cetera et cetera."

"I was restrained," I told her.

"Because they flew airplanes, so many of them. If they weren't pilots, you would've thought they were the King's Guards or something, servants of Demon Drugs damned to hell. But because they fly airplanes you saw them as people like you, and you didn't shout *Die Druggie Whitecoats,* not once!"

"No. I am a naturally courteous person."

"Unless you're threatened," she said. "And you weren't when you saw they loved flying, too."

"Well, yes."

"Three: I Liked Our Little Talk About Home. I really have felt like an outsider, most of my life. Not because I moved a lot, but because I am an outsider. I don't think the way they do where I grew up, I don't think like my mom or my dad or anybody in my family."

"You do think the same as your family, sweetie," I told her. "Only your family isn't who you thought they were."

"I guess you're right," she said. "Till I found that out, I was pretty lonely. Then I found you."

"Me?" I said, astonished. "You *married* amanwhoisin-manyways your *brother?*"

"I'd do it again," she said, unashamed. "How many people are there, Richie, who think they're odd and different and lonely outsiders, when all that's happened is they haven't met their family?"

"Unless we've been odd and different," I said, "unless we've been away, we'll never have the fun of coming home."

"There's home again. Tell me what's home, to you?"

When I started the sentence, I didn't know how it would end. "Home, I think, is the known and loved." I felt it click inside, the way every real answer clicks in mind. "Isn't it true? You sit down at the piano, just to play for yourself, you know the music and you love it, isn't that coming home? I sit at the controls of a little airplane, there's home for me. We're together, you and me, so right now home's in a moving automobile; next month it could be some different city. When we're together, we're home."

"Home's not in the stars?"

"Home isn't place. Known and loved, I don't think, aren't nailed or roofed or planted. We can become attached to nails and roofs, but shift their order from known to un and when we come back we say what's this pile of sticks? Home is a certain *order* that's dear to us, where it's safe to be who we are."

"That's very nice, Wookie," she said.

"And I'll bet that before we choose a life on earth there's some loved known order from which we come, that's got nothing to do with time and distance, that's got no molecules at all!"

"And just because we're here doesn't mean we've forgotten," she said. "Don't you have those times, sweetie, have you had them, when you . . . almost . . . remember?"

"Sixth grade!" And that moment, driving with my wife, no sign of Dickie, it was with me as though it had never left.

Twenty-one

"Sixth grade was a crowd, Leslie, what was I doing in a crowd?"

Ranch gone, water tower a memory, the sea of sage and rock flickered to become a sea of tidy houses, grass-color suburbs drifting on the slow tide of California.

So many children at school, I thought. Not one can saddle and bridle a burro, yet somehow these are not bad people, most of them. Limited, but not bad.

In turn, they looked at me curious for a few days, but coming to California from Arizona did not rate with coming from New York or Belgium. I was harmless, not so different from themselves, and in time, losing novelty, I was accepted, one more chip in the currents.

"Budgie, am I crazy?"

"Yes."

We cruised slowly down the empty autumn street, after-school bicycles pedaled side by side, fat tires crunching sycamore leaves.

"Don't say yes until I tell you how I think I'm crazy, because if I am you are, too."

"You're not crazy."

There may have been somebody smarter than Anthony Zerbe in the Mark Twain Elementary School but I doubted it. For sure there was no one quicker of mind, or stronger or faster on his feet or better to have on your side when you were in trouble.

"Are you a child, Budgie?" I asked.

"Yes. Technically, I'm a child. You and I are children."

"Exactly! Technically is right. But inside, are you a child? Inside, do you *feel* like a child?"

"Of course not," he said, folding his arms and riding no-hands, pulling half a length ahead of me, coasting a second till I caught up. "My mind's more adult than some adults I know. Need I mention . . . Mr. Anderson? But my body hasn't caught up. I don't know how to earn money or get married or buy houses. I'm not tall enough.

There's a lot of information I need and I don't have it yet. But inside, as a person, I'm grown-up."

"So do you figure that the reason we're children is not because we're worthless but because we need time to get that information, and get taller, and when we're grown-ups we're going to feel just the way we do now except we'll know more nuts and bolts about how to get along?"

"Bet you're right," he said, unconcerned. "Inside, we'll feel same as we do now."

"Doesn't that bother you?"

"Why?"

"We're the same as grown-up, but we're powerless, Budge! Don't you hate being powerless? Don't you want to get on with it?"

"No. I'm powerless but unlike you, I'm . . ."

He stopped midsentence, and down the gentle hill on Blackthorne Street, he lifted his feet to the handlebars, coasted while our speed increased.

"Unlike me you're what?"

"I'm patient!" he said over the wind. "I don't mind my dad has to earn the money, and not me. I don't mind being a child. There's a lot to learn. Just the nuts and bolts, there's a lot to learn!"

"I do mind. I want to get on with it. If I'm grown-up inside . . . they ought to make it that if you pass a test you're a licensed adult, doesn't matter how many years you have or don't have."

"All in good time," he said.

My friend put his feet back on the pedals, grabbed the handlebars, swerved to the curb and last instant before impact he jerked his front wheel a foot off the ground, hopped the bicycle onto the sidewalk. Forgotten, the days when bicycles terrified me, when I ran to Mom for protection after Roy swung me on the high seat and pushed, threatened to let me coast alone.

I angled onto the walk behind Zerbe via the next driveway, absorbed in the difference between us.

"Don't you think you're somebody special?"

"Aha!" he said, swinging midspeed off the bike to run alongside for a moment, stopping on the grass of his front lawn. "Don't you?"

I stopped too, stayed on the pedals till the bike began to topple from under me, then jumped off and laid it down on the grass.

"Of course I'm somebody special," I said. "Everybody's somebody special! Name me someone in our class, name me anybody at Mark Twain Elementary School who's planning to grow up and be a failure!"

Zerbe sat cross-legged on the lawn, leaned against the seat of his bicycle. "But it happens, doesn't it? Something happens between now when we know we're special and then when we say I guess not and turn into a failure."

"It's not going to happen to me," I said.

He laughed. "How do you know? What makes you so sure? Maybe we're not really grown-up. Maybe we're only grown-up when we know we're *not* somebody special. Maybe failure is a job only real grown-ups can handle."

"Like heck!" I said. "We may be kids, but inside we're already finished, and we're not just . . . nothing!"

"Go on," he said. "I'm not against you. Tell me. How do you know you're somebody special?"

"Mornings," I told him. "Sometimes mornings I wake up and go outside and the air is so . . . *green,* do you understand? The air is saying *Something's going to happen today! Something powerful is going to happen!* And it never quite happens, as far as I can tell, but there's that feeling in the air. It doesn't happen, but it happens. You don't know what I'm saying, do you?"

"Maybe you're just wishing something would happen."

"I don't make this up, Budge! I swear I don't make it up. There's something out there and it's like . . . it's sort of calling to me. You hear it too, don't you? I don't mean hear, but you feel it sometimes, don't you?"

He looked me straight in the eyes. "It's a light inside me," he said, "like I swallowed a star."

"YES! And cut somebody open you're never going to find that star, you're never going to find it with a microscope big as a house!"

My friend lay against his bike and watched twilight through the trees. "You can't see stars in the daytime. You have to close your eyes, kind of adjust to the dark and you see this faint light way far away. Is that what you see, Dick?"

Only friends dare talk like this, I thought. "The light's a silver chain, like an anchor-chain in my mind, going out of sight down into deep water."

"Deep water!" he said. "Right-O! And we're divers, gliding down, and way way deep the chain leads to this sunken star. That's our anchor . . ."

I was a dolphin burst high into the air from a prison-tank, come down in the open sea to find a mirror friend alongside. I wasn't the only one knew Something was tugging on us from beyond words!

"You know it, Budge! An anchor of light! I swim down there, and no matter how bad anything is, everything's okay. I'm way deep underwater, my boat's out of sight on the surface, but that anchor's brighter than flashbulbs ever were and it's inside me!"

"Yeah." He sighed, smile gone, wistful. "It's there, all right."

"Well, what are you going to *do* about it? You know that . . . light . . . is down there and what do you do about it?"

"I guess I'll wait."

"You'll *wait*? Holy cow, Budge, how can you know it's there and *wait*?" I hoped he knew that was frustration in my voice, not anger.

"What else can I do? What do you do, Dick, on your green mornings?" He picked a blade of crabgrass, chewed the hard clean stem.

"I want to run. It's like there's some place right nearby that if I knew where to run there would be this spaceship hidden, with the door open, and somebody's there who knows who I am, they've been gone for a long time

131

they're coming to pick me up and the door goes shhhhhhh and closes and mmmmmmmm the ship lifts off and there's my house down below but nobody can see me or see the ship and it just lifts up and up and there I am in the stars, going home."

My friend spun his bike's front wheel with a finger, slow empty roulette. "That's why you ask if you're crazy?"

"A little bit."

"Well," he said, "you're crazy, all right."

"I am. You, too."

"Not me," he said.

"Tell me again about swallowing stars, please."

He laughed. "I'll deny that to anybody but you."

"Thanks."

"And you'd better deny it, too," he said. "Or at least not talk it much around."

"You think I talk this to everybody?" I said. "I never will again. But we are special, you know that too, don't you? Not just you and me. Everybody."

132

"Until we grow up," he said.

"Oh, come on, Budgie. You don't believe that."

He stood in the dim light, lifted his bicycle upright, rolled it toward his back yard.

"Really. Don't be in such a hurry," he said. "This whole thing takes time. If you want to remember who you are, you'd better find a way not to grow up."

Riding home in the dark, I thought about that. Maybe my spaceship wouldn't find me. Maybe I had to find it.

✦

Leslie turned the wheel, listening, angled the car to an off-ramp, paused at the stop sign, pressed on down the wide suburban street.

"You've never told me that," she said. "Just when I think I'm getting to know you, you come up with something like this."

"May you never know me. I'll remember more, if you ask."

"Really? Tell me."

"The green times! Every once in a while, I knew how everything worked, why I was who I was, where I was, what was going to happen. I didn't know in words. I knew in feelings, it felt yes, this was what I asked for and now here I am on this little planet in the middle of seems-to-be. Pull back the curtain and there's home, just a turn of mind away."

"But the curtain closed again, didn't it?" she said. "It did for me."

"Yeah. It always closed again, like the roof closing over my own private movie theater, and there I was in the dark again and the only thing in sight was my life going on, two dimensions but looking like four."

I felt the kid in my mind, listening as I spoke. "Once in Florida, in the Air Force, walking back to the barracks after night flying, I looked up and there was this huge curtain, like the whole Milky Way galaxy pulled to one side for about half a minute and I slammed to a stop, stood frozen, watching the sky."

"What was on the other side?" she said. "What did you see?"

"Nothing! Isn't that strange? What I saw was this luminous veil just swept away, and in its place was not a sight but a feeling of tremendous joy: *It's All Right. Everything's All Right.* Then the veil drifted back again and there were the stars, same as ever, and me standing there in the dark."

I looked at her, remembering. "That feeling never left, Wookie. To this minute, it's never quite disappeared."

"I've seen you awfully mad, sweetie," she said. "I've seen you where I'd have sworn you didn't think everything was all right."

"Sure enough. But isn't it the same for you: it's like you're playing pickle-ball, and you get so carried away in the play that you forget it's a game?"

"There are a lot of times I forget it's a game," she said. "I think real life is real, and I think you do, too."

"Looks that way sometimes, I'll admit. I get frustrated, something stands in my way. Or I'll get angry which is to say frightened when what I want to do or who I want to be is threatened. But that's a mood of the game. Take me out of the game, tell me in my angriest minute, *Your life is over, Richard, spacetime has just stopped,* and anger's gone, whatever it was doesn't matter anymore, I'm me again."

"Let me remember that line," she said. *"Your life is over . . ."*

I laughed, knowing I'd hear those words the next time I lost my temper. "Instant perspective, is all it is. Do you think so?"

She wheeled the car around the corner, up the drive to

our house. Love lasts in a marriage, I thought, as long as wife and husband keep caring about what the other thinks.

She stopped the car, turned off the engine. "That's what he wants, isn't it?" she said.

"Who?"

"Dickie. He wants instant perspective. Whatever happens, he wants to know it's all right."

Twenty-two

*I*t must have rained in his desert, for the dry lake-bed had turned to grass, mere tracings where the fault lines of his memories had been. There was a tree on the near horizon. How could it change so fast?

He stood clear across the lake, at the foot of a gentle hill, and I jogged to meet him. "Were you there, Captain?" I asked.

"At the ball?" he said. "When you were scared? Yes."

"I wasn't scared."

"You didn't mind me figuring out your escape, in case they had the Aspirin Toast . . ."

"A fine escape, Dickie. I was almost hoping for the Toast."

"Thank you," he said. "It would have worked."

"Yes. There would have been consequences."

"My job is to get you out of there. Consequences are for grown-ups."

"No consequences required," I said. "I could have walked out the same way I walked in. No explanations, just leave because I didn't feel like being there. No chase, no commotion, no wrecked drapes, no shattered glass, no climbing up gargoyles six stories over the sidewalk in my street shoes, no how do I get off the rooftops and back to Leslie. No consequences."

He shrugged. "So you're a grown-up."

"You're right," I said. "It would have worked, it would have been a great scene."

He set off walking up the hill, as though there was something up there he wanted to show me.

"Do you really not believe in medicine?" he said.

"Really."

"Not even aspirin."

I shook my head. "Nope."

"What about when you're sick?"

"I don't get sick," I said.

"Never?"

"Almost never."

"What do you do when you're sick?" he asked.

"I crawl back from the drugstore dragging carts of medicine. I start with acetaminophen and I don't stop swallowing till the Zantac's gone."

"If your body's a perfect expression of your thought about body," he said, "why are you bald as a cue-ball? Why do you use glasses to read maps, when you're flying?"

"*I AM NOT BALD AS A CUE-BALL!*" I told him. "My thought about body includes that I decided to make my hair a little more manageable now than it used to be, that it's all right for fine print to look blurry and for me to peer at it through glass and think it's sharper. Did I catch that thought from noticing every day when I was you that Dad's hair was thinner than mine, that Dad and Mom wore glasses to read?"

He didn't answer.

"Just because I know my body's a mirror of my

thought," I said, "doesn't mean I'm not lazy, that I don't let my beliefs go the easy way. The minute my body-image seriously bothers me, when it's top priority to change, I'll change."

"What if you're really sick?" he said. "No kidding."

"Doesn't happen. Once maybe in years and years. When I learned to fly, I was convinced that airplane pilots never get sick. It's true. I don't know anybody who flies who's very often ill."

He looked at me askance. "Why?"

How come we don't know answers until we find the question, I thought. Before I opened my mouth, I hadn't a clue why aviators are a healthy lot.

"Flying's still a fantasy," I said, "for a lot of us. How many fantasies include disease? Live enough of what you've always dreamed of doing and there's no room left for feeling bad."

He smiled, hiking up the hill, as though he'd been reading my mind. "You're kidding, Richard," he said. "You're just like Dad. You're kidding and you do it with this oh-so-serious face so I can never tell."

"Don't believe me. Learn for yourself, Captain. There's a study somewhere, compares the health of people doing

140

what they love to do against the condition of the working miserable. Who do you think's better off?"

"I can guess."

I touched his shoulder as we hiked. "What if there's no study?" I said. "Does that make your guess less true?"

He flashed a grin to me, a look completely unguarded.

"It's called a thought experiment," I told him. "It's a way to find out what you already know."

"Thought experiment!" he said. "Neat!"

"You want answers?"

"Come on, Richard. Yes!"

"No," I said.

"Why don't I want answers!"

"Because answers change," I said. "You don't want a million answers as much as you want a few forever questions. The questions are diamonds you hold in the light. Study a lifetime and you see different colors from the same jewel. The same questions, asked again, bring you just the answers you need just the minute you need them."

141

He frowned, fixing his eyes on the hilltop as he climbed. "Questions like what?"

"Questions like *Who am I?*"

He was unimpressed. "For instance."

"For instance, let's say you've got a problem. Everybody else in school will do anything to be popular. Will you? Will you wear fad clothes, wear fad judgments and prejudices and attitudes so you can be safe and same?"

"I don't know. I want to have friends . . ."

"And that's your problem. So you find a bubble of quiet and you ask yourself, *who am I?*"

With the climb, we could see farther over the green-velvet desert. Was my inner landscape greening up too, for finding this child and wanting him free?

"Who am I," he said. "Then what?"

"Then you listen. And listening, you remember. Who you are is someone who asked to be dropped off on earth so you could do something remarkable, something that mattered to you. Does Something Remarkable mean you slop up every dumb belief of every thoughtless popular nobody to pretend you have friends?"

"Well . . ."

"*Who am I* doesn't wear out, Dickie. It helps you choose what to do, time after time, your whole life long."

"Who are my friends?"

"You've got it!" I said, proud of him.

He stopped climbing and looked at me. "I've got what?"

"*Who are my friends?* There's a question to last! Next time you surround yourself with a dozen lost sheep worshiping the cut of your big-league jacket and your way-in haircut and your super-cool sunglasses, ask. Who are my friends, my real friends, who are the others who came from the stars? Where are they now and what are they doing? Am I being my own friend, poisoning my starmind with dead sludge conformity, lifting a glass of Killer Lite with the guys?"

Dickie reached a calming hand to mine. "Richard, I'm just a kid . . ."

"Anyway," I grumbled as we resumed our climb. "You get the point. Remember who you are and there's your answer. What's a star-person doing mucking in swamp values?"

He smiled at me. "Would it bother you, Richard, if I decide to be a drunk?"

I turned to him, startled. "Dickie?"

"Let's say I turn out to be a *cigarette-smoking pill-eating flag-waving Bible-thumping macho party-animal we're-number-one womanizing drunk,*" he said. "Would that bother you?"

"If you made those choices, Captain, not many women would touch you with a stick. You can cross off womanizing."

"Just let's say I did," he said. "What would you think?"

For a moment, off balance, was I annoyed? Anger is always fear, I thought, and fear is always fear of loss. Would I lose myself if he made those choices? It took a second to settle down: I'd lose nothing. They'd be his wishes, not mine, and he's free to live as he wants. The loss would come if I dared force him, tried to live for him and me as well. There'd be disaster worse than life on a bar stool.

It took that moment and that idea to vaporize annoyance, for me to relax again.

"The only qualities you've missed," I said sternly, "are *judgmental* and *controlling*. They're mine and you can't have them. Otherwise I think your life is your right to live."

"You wouldn't feel bad about me?"

"I can't be distressed over what I don't control," I said. "But I'll tell you what, Dickie. You give me authority over your life, you follow my directions to the letter, you think and say and do nothing but what I tell you to, and I'll be responsible for your life."

"I won't be Captain?"

"Nope," I said. "I take command."

"Success guaranteed?"

"No guarantees. But if I wreck your life I promise to feel bad about it."

He stopped in his tracks. "What? You take over, you make my decisions for me, I follow all your directions and when you smash my ship on the rocks you promise to *feel bad*? If it's my life getting wrecked, I'll steer it myself, thank you!"

I smiled at him. "The beginning of wisdom, Captain."

When we reached the top of the hill, he stopped by a crude wooden seatback pounded into the earth. I could understand why he might choose this place to sit: it was the closest he could come to flying without wings or a dream.

"Pretty view," I said. "Springtime in your country?"

A shy smile. "The season comes slowly."

Why don't I tell him straight, I thought. Why don't I just tell him that I love him and I'll be his friend for as long as I live? Do the meanings of the heart swim in the streams of our conversation, and do they matter most when they're glimpsed through deep water, and never caught?

"I guess it takes a little rain," I said.

"A little," he said. For a moment he looked to the far distance, as though he were gathering courage. Then he turned to me. "Your country needs rain, too, Richard."

"Maybe so." What did he have in mind? It's a pleasure to give him the gift of whatever I've learned, I thought, no payment required.

"I'm not sure what this means to you," he said, "but it probably means a lot."

Before I could ask what he had in mind, he wrestled the wooden seatback wildly side to side, finally broke it loose from the ground and handed it to me, child Moses handing a faded tablet.

It wasn't a seatback, it was a grave-board, a homemade

146

tombstone. Carved in the wood was no date, no epitaph. Four words only:

Bobby Bach
My Brother

Half a century safely forgotten, it all came back.

Twenty-three

"Why are you so smart?"

My brother glanced up from his book, looked down the year and a half between us, his eyes testing mine. "What are you talking about, Dickie? I'm not so smart."

I thought about that, and he went back to reading.

"Everybody says you're smart, Bobby."

Any other brother would turn cross, tell the seven-year-old get lost. For some reason, mine didn't mind.

"Okay, they're right," he said. "I have to be smart because I've got to go ahead, I've got to lead the way for you."

If he was kidding, he didn't let it show.

"Did Roy lead the way for you?"

He put his book down for a moment. "No. Roy's nearly grown up, and Roy's different. I'm no good at designing things or putting things together. I can't draw the way Roy can draw."

"Me neither."

"But we can read together, can't we?" He slid to one side of the big chair. "Want to practice your reading?"

I climbed up beside him. "Is that why you're smart, because you read so much?"

"No. I read so much because I have to stay ahead of you. If I'm going to lead the way, I have to stay ahead, don't I?" He flattened the book out on our laps. "I just hope you can't read this book already! You couldn't be that smart, could you?"

I looked at the pages, very smart indeed, and smiled. "Oh, yes I could . . ."

He pointed at the capital letters. "What does this say?"

"Easy," I told him. *"CHAPTER THIRTEEN. BE-YOND THE SOLAR SYSTEM."*

"Good! Read me the first paragraph."

A child could earn a lot of praise in our household, but the quickest compliment came from reading well, "with expression," as Mom would say. Turn printed words into spoken and you were an excellent son.

So I read to my brother that day, trying my best to sound as if I were telling him about the stars instead of reading about them. But settling deep within me were the words I took for truth: "I've got to lead the way for you."

✦

Home from school, through the gate hungry, open the back door to the kitchen. With luck I could sneak three or four pieces of rye bread that if Mom saw me would spoil my dinner.

Yike . . . Dad's home from work early, sitting with Mom and Bobby at the kitchen table.

They were talking seriously, quietly together as though my brother were some guest instead of their son. This has never happened. My father, home *early*?

"Hi, Daddy," I said, not a hint I was frightened. "Are we going to move again? Something important going to happen? Is this a conference going on?"

"We're talking with Bobby," said my father. "And I think we'd like to be alone. Is that all right?"

I stared at him for most of a second, glanced at Mom. She looked at me solemnly, spoke not a word. Something was terribly wrong.

"Okay," I said, "sure. I'll be over at Mike's. See you later."

I pushed through the swinging door from the kitchen into the living room, let it close behind me, walked out the front door.

What in the heck is happening? They've never had any kind of talk that I can't at least listen to. I'm part of this family, aren't I? Maybe I'm not! Are they deciding to get rid of me? Why?

Next door to Mike's house grew the best climbing-tree I knew, an evergreen with limbs like spiral-ladder rungs all the way to the top, so many of them there was no way to fall. If you could reach those first heavy branches, six feet in the air, the rest was easy.

What could they possibly be saying? Why didn't they want me to hear?

A running jump. Tennis shoes gripped the bark, slid and caught, one more half-jump and the branch was made. I disappeared in heavy boughs, resolute, climbing steadily.

Whatever they're talking about, it's not something nice,

it's not a surprise for me. They would have just stopped talking, or changed the subject when I walked in, talked about the office or the Bible or something.

Toward the top of the tree the branches were smaller, patches of view out over the housetops. The view was best up there, but the limbs were twigs, the trunk itself just inches thick, easy to sway.

I quit climbing short of the top . . . this was no devil's dare, I needed to think, and here was the alonest place I knew.

Mom always asks me how was school, I thought, what did I learn today? I wanted to tell her I learned about the Law of Averages, what does she know about how it works, but suddenly she doesn't care. And why is Dad home at this hour? Has somebody died? What could be so wrong?

The only person I had ever known who had died was my grandmother, and they told me when it happened. I had met her once, stern and white-haired, barely taller than me, and I didn't cry that she was gone. Neither did Mom cry, nor Dad, of course.

Nobody's died. They'd have told me.

A quarter of a mile away, most of my house was hidden by tree-needles, but I could make out part of the roof over the kitchen. Not hard to tell. Everybody else in Lakewood Village had a sloping roof, mine was flat.

What was going on over there?

A breath of wind swept the tree, rocked it gently. I locked an arm around the trunk.

It had to be something about me, I thought, else why was it so important for me to leave? It has something to do with me, and it is not good.

That's not possible. Even when the principal calls me to his office, it's something good: congratulations you've been chosen fire monitor; would you think of running for school office; you scored higher on the state test than any-one except your brother.

Twilight found me clinging, a worried raccoon in the tree, still deep in the dark for all my concern, anxious but determined never to ask. I'll let them tell me what's going on at whatever time they decide to tell me. I'm helpless. There's nothing I can do. It's something big, it's something I'm not supposed to know, and that's that.

I slipped down the trunk and walked home, rubbing spots of pine tar into my jeans.

When I pushed through the swinging door into the kitchen, Dad was gone, Mom was cooking dinner. Not only dinner, but she was sliding a schaumtort into the oven.

"Hi, Dickie," she said, her sparkle gone. "What did you learn in school today?"

I gave in to her mood, matched it. "Nothing," I said.

✦

Bobby missed school more often, and those private meetings happened again from time to time.

Alone in the bedroom that he and I shared, I heard quiet voices through the wall sometimes, mostly Dad's, sometimes Mom's, and Bobby's so rarely or so softly that I wasn't sure he spoke.

Once, bedtime, as he climbed the ladder to the upper bunk, I broke my resolve.

"What's going on, Bobby?" I said. "With Mom and Dad. What do you talk about? Is it something about me?"

He didn't look over the edge at me, as he sometimes did. "It's a secret," he said. "It's not about you. It's nothing you need to know."

✦

We could almost always talk, Bobby and me, and now we couldn't. At least they're not going to come for me in

154

the night, throw me blindfolded in the back of a truck and cart me off to hell. Maybe my brother was kidding. Maybe they are coming for me. But if he won't tell, he won't tell.

Next day I found a soft-leather bag on the desk in our room, the size of a pirate's money-pouch. Never seen this before . . .

When I loosened the thongs and opened the bag I found not gold inside but an idol. Fine-crafted of polished ebony, it was the figure of a laughing Buddha, arms overhead, palms up, fingertips nearly touching. What in the heck . . .

Footsteps. Bobby's coming! I stuffed the figure back into the pouch, drew it shut, threw myself onto my bed and opened a book, *Rockets, Missiles and Space Travel,* by Willy Ley.

"Hi, Bobby." I looked up when he entered, went back to reading.

"Hi."

I read intently, memorized in that moment what I recall today: solid-fuel rocket engines aren't crammed full of powder, they're packed around a conical firing chamber. The bigger the burning area, the more thrust. Too big, I bet, and the rocket explodes VOOM! like dynamite.

"See you later," my brother said, and he was gone, taking his coat and the leather pouch, off someplace in the car with Dad.

✦

Two weeks later, Bobby, looking tired, drove with Dad to the hospital, nothing serious.

In a week, no good-byes, my brother was dead.

Of course, I thought, nine-year-old Holmes of Baker Street, that was the secret! Of course the long quiet talks alone: everybody knew Bobby was dying except me! It was their way to keep me from pain.

The ebony Buddha was reaching for answers, and I couldn't guess whether my brother had found them.

He could have told me, I wouldn't have felt sad. I could have asked what dying feels like, does it hurt? Where do you go when you die, Bobby, can you not-die if you don't want to do it? Do angels come to visit in your sleep? Is dying as neat as it sounds? Are you scared?

As far as I knew, Mom didn't cry, Roy didn't cry, Dad certainly didn't. So neither did I, not that anyone could see. The only change was that it was awfully quiet, alone in the bedroom.

The Long Beach *Press-Telegram* carried a small obituary,

said Bobby was survived by Dad and Mom and Roy and me. I stuck the clipping to my door with a model-airplane pin, glamoured that a newspaper noticed and put our names in print.

The next day the clipping came loose; I found it face-down on my desk. I pinned it up again, and the next day it was back down. I took the hint. Mom may not be crying, but she'd just as soon not be reminded by newspapers that Bobby was dead.

✦

She told me at last, drying dishes, sliding them, slow gentle clank of china plate, into the cupboard. "Bobby had leukemia."

I memorized the word instantly.

"There's no cure. The last days, Dick, he was so calm about it all. He was so wise!"

No tears, and she had changed my name from Dickie.

" 'Everything has its place, Mom,' he told me. 'It's my place to die now. I'm not afraid, please don't be sad, don't grieve for me, I couldn't stand it if you cried.' "

A tear spilled, and the talk was over.

I had been one lucky boy, all right. What safer life than

to fly easy and comfortable behind my brother? He leads, I follow.

Now instead of level flight and gentle turns ahead of me, Bobby had crammed on full power, pulled straight up and disappeared into the sun.

My heart was terrified. I sobbed under the blankets at night, yelled into the pillow. *Please, Bobby, PLEASE! Don't leave me here alone! You promised to show me the way! You promised! Don't go! I don't know how to live without my brother!*

Crying does zero good, I found out. Feelings don't change things. It's knowing that matters, and I've got a lot to learn.

I looked up *death* in the dictionary: formal statements of the obvious.

I read the encyclopedia: no answer.

Bobby had been so serene, I thought, so unfrightened. It was as though he had chosen to stride eyes open into dying, as though he had been training for a test. When the test came, when the door opened, he squared his shoulders and he walked straight through, head up, no looking back.

Well done, brother, I thought, thanks for showing me the way.

But you know something else, Bobby? All of a sudden I've changed, all of a sudden I'm a competitive son of a bitch and I'm damned if I'm gonna die before I know why I lived.

The boy who cried his terror after his brother, I let him go that day, left him there alone and went on to live without him.

Twenty-four

Dickie took the grave-board from my hands.

"Tell me again," he said. "What does *meaning* mean?"

I blinked at him. Just relived one of the most wrenching moments of my life, relived thanks to him in vivid pain, now he's turned into some cold stranger?

He answered my thought. "Why not? That's what you did."

"Thanks for the balance," I said.

"You know your answer. What does *meaning* mean?"

I turned dispassionate, a change that comes easy with practice, and told him. "Meaning, to me, is whatever changes our thought, and therefore changes our lives."

"What does Bobby's death mean to you?" He jammed

the grave-board back into the dirt from which it had come. It fell over as soon as he moved his hand away. "How did it change your life?"

"I never knew till now. Stuffed it away and forgot."

He tried again with the board, and this time when it fell over he let it lie.

"What does it mean?"

The moment he asked, I knew. Pulling that hidden memory free was pulling the keypole from a logjam, and the current beneath was swift.

"Bobby's death for the first time in my life threw me *on my own*. For a half century now I've thought I've always been on my own, I blotted out the time before. Wrong! When I was you, Bobby promised that he'd make the discoveries, he'd take the shocks of living before they got to me. He'd soften them, explain them so my way would be easy, paved through the wilderness. All I had to do was follow my brother and everything would turn out fine."

He sat quietly in the grass, I paced back and forth nearby, a greyhound restless to run. "That day, everything changed. When Bobby died, his brother the wagon-passenger had to mount up right quick and learn to be his own frontier scout."

Back over my life I flew, top speed, looking down. "Everything I learned, Dickie, from that moment on, taught me the power of the individual to change destiny, the power of individual choice. Everything that happened after: Roy joined the army, Dad stayed distant, Mom went into politics, I learned to fly airplanes . . . every one taught trust of self, every one said never expect someone else to show you the way or to make you happy."

He looked at the far horizon. "Mom and Dad don't think that way."

"That's right. They thought the opposite. Mom the missionary, the social worker, the councilwoman; Dad the minister, the chaplain, the Red Cross manager. They taught Live for Others, and Dickie, they were wrong!"

He stiffened. "Don't tell me Mom's wrong," he growled. "You can say she's different, Richard, but don't you ever tell me that Mom is wrong!"

How much I had loved my mother, and how little her values had touched me! Live for others, Mom, it's the worst possible blow to the ones you want to help. Pull their wagons up mountains for them and you're the one winds up with a broken heart. You shielded me from Bobby's death, saved me from my feelings, and it's fifty years before I face them on my own. How could you have been so wrong, and why do I love you still?

"I'm glad she didn't tell me that Bobby was going to die," I said. "I cannot imagine, I am unable to bend my mind enough to suspect who I might possibly have become today if she had."

"A missionary?" he said.

"Me a missionary? Impossible! Probably so."

"Could you be a missionary now?" He said that as if he hoped it might posthumously comfort my mother.

I laughed out loud. "It's the priest who killed God for me, Dickie! Don't you remember?"

"No."

Of course, I thought. He's the Keeper of the Forgotten, and this I remember like today.

"After Bobby died," I said, "in my simple surviving-child questions to the inner priest waited the destruction of God-as-I-knew-Him, and my first glimpse of my own truth."

Dickie couldn't imagine I remembered anything significant from my childhood. "What priest? What happened?"

"I'll show you what happened," I said. "When I stand

163

here, I'll be me. When I stand there, I'll be the Inner Priest. Okay?"

He smiled, anticipating some fast scrambling on the hilltop.

" 'Is God all-powerful?' I ask, little child to knowing elder."

I stepped ahead and turned to look down upon the child I had been. I was a jolly priest, now, dark green robe, company logo on a chain around my neck. " 'Of course! Otherwise He'd not be God, would He, son?'

" 'Does God love us?'

" 'How can you ask? God loves us, every one!'

" 'Why do nice people who God loves get killed in wars and cruelty, in senseless murder and stupid accidents, why do innocent smart children suffer to death without mercy, why did my brother die?' "

Careful with the voice now, a gentle mask for ignorance. " 'Some things are beyond knowing, my child. The Father sends the greatest evil to those He loves the most. He needs to be sure you care for Him more than your mortal brother. Have faith and trust in Almighty God . . .'

164

" 'ARE YOU GONE HOG-STUPID CRAZY??
YOU THINK I'M A NINE-YEAR-OLD IDIOT?
EITHER ADMIT THAT GOD IS NO MORE AL-
MIGHTY THAN I AM, THAT THE GUY'S
MARSHMALLOW-HELPLESS AGAINST EVIL,
OR ELSE ADMIT THAT WHAT GOD CALLS
LOVE WE CALL WICKED SADIST HATRED
FROM THE BLOODIEST MASS MURDERER
EVER PULLED AN AXE!'

" 'Okay,' says the padre, all sudden candor. 'I'm
wrong, you're right. I offered you comfort, you had
to have truth. Like so many children, you have just
demolished organized religion, Mr. Rational Seeker.
You know I can't answer those questions, no priest
can. And now you'll have to design your religion for
yourself.'

" 'Why?' says I. 'I don't need religion. I'll do without.'

" 'And leave the mystery of why we're here unsolved?'

"To leave it unsolved," I told Dickie offstage, "would
have been to admit that there was something I couldn't
figure out. And I knew that if I wanted enough to know,
there was nothing I couldn't understand. That, for openers,
would be the first tenet of my new religion."

I returned to my little play.

"'It'll be easy,' says I. 'Any child can come up with something better than a slaughterhouse for a world and God with knives in his hands.'

"'There's a price to pay,' warns the priest. 'Design your own theology and you'll be different from everyone else . . .'

"'That's no price,' scoffs I, 'that's a reward! And besides, nobody really believes, do they, in God-the-Powerless or God-the-Killer? It'll be easy.'

"My inner padre smiles at that, a superior smile, and disappears."

Dickie watched, absorbed in my theatrics.

"As soon as he left," I said, "I got nervous. Had I been impetuous and emotional in my little outburst? Cool and careful over the next ten years, I put it back together, no italics, no exclamation points. It took that long to fit the pieces, but the foundation was finished. Thanks to my brother, I had rebuilt God. Help me with this, Dickie, show me where I'm wrong."

He nodded, eager to be a part of a home-made religion.

"Pretend there lives an All-Powerful God who sees mortals and their troubles on earth," I said slowly.

He nodded.

"Then, Dickie, God must be responsible for all the catastrophe, tragedy, terror and death that besets humanity."

He raised his hand. "Just because God sees our troubles, He's not responsible for them."

"Think carefully. Because He's *all-powerful*. That is, He has the power to stop the bad stuff if He wants to. But He chooses not to stop it. By allowing evil to exist, He's the reason that it's there."

He thought about that. "Maybe . . ." he said carefully.

"By definition, then, because the innocent continue to suffer and die, an all-powerful God is not just uncaring, He's unspeakably cruel."

Dickie raised his hand again, more for time to follow than to ask a question. "Maybe . . ."

"You're not sure," I said.

"It sounds weird, but I can't see where it's wrong."

"I can't, either. Is the world changing for you on that thought, the way it did for me . . . a wicked cruel God?"

"Go on," he said.

"Next. Pretend there's an All-*Loving* God who sees mortals and knows their troubles on earth."

"That's better."

I nodded. "Then this God must watch in sorrow as the innocent are oppressed and murdered by the evil time and again, murdered by the millions as they pray in vain for help, century after century . . ."

He raised his hand. "Next you're going to say this: Because the innocent suffer and die, our all-loving God has no power to help us."

"Exactly! Tell me when you're ready for a question."

He took a moment, went over what we had said. Then he nodded. "Okay. I'm ready for your question."

"Which God is real, Dickie?" I asked. "The cruel one or the powerless?"

Twenty-five

*H*e considered for the longest time, then laughed, thinking about it, shook his head. "That's no choice! I mean if the choice is Cruel or Powerless, then to heck with God!"

Watching him, I saw what I must have looked like, years past, figuring it out. "The choice is no choice," I said. "Neither one is real."

"Back at the beginning," he said, "was there something wrong with the question?"

Had I noticed so much when I was him? "Good! What makes the choice unreal, Dickie, is the question: Pretend there's a God *who sees mortals and knows their troubles on earth*. Fold it any way you want, I did for years, but the minute you imagine that God sees us as mortals in trouble, there's no way to avoid having to choose one or the other, Cruel or Powerless."

"What's left?" he said. "There's no God?"

"If you insist that spacetime is real . . . that spacetime always has been and always will be, there's either no God or you get the choice above."

"What if I don't insist spacetime is real?"

I picked a stone from the ground and threw it low, skimmed it off the air above the hilltop and far down the slope. I remembered the moment when I decided not to insist, just for the fun of it.

"I don't know," I said.

"Oh, come on!" He pulled a clod of earth by the grass-stems and threw it, aiming to miss. "You do so know!"

"Think about it, we'll figure that out next time."

"You better not leave now, Richard! WHERE'S MY FLAMETHROWER?"

"Do you know, Dickie, this would be a great hill for paragliding? Wind's from the south, usually?"

"There's no wind here unless I say so," he said, "and

now that you've just killed God I say you'd better raise Him from the dead or I promise you are gonna get no sleep!"

"Okay. But I can't raise Him from the dead because He isn't a Him."

"He's a She?"

"She's an Is," I said.

"Ready, go," he said, giving me back my stage.

"Okay. I withdraw my consent from a God either helpless or unwilling to overcome evil. I do not withdraw my consent from an all-powerful all-loving reality."

"Then you're right back where you started!"

"No. Listen. It's simple." I drew an outline in air. "Here's a door. On the door are two words. *Life Is.* If you walk through the door, you see the world in which that's true."

"I don't have to believe that Life Is," he said, determined not to be caught again by assumptions.

"No, you don't. If you don't believe that, or if you believe *Life Isn't,* or *Life Sometimes Is and Sometimes Isn't,* or *Death Is,* then the world has to be pretty well what it seems

171

to be, forget purpose and sense. We're all on our own, some are born lucky, others cry a lot before they die, no telling which is which. Good luck.''

I waited for him, while he tapped on those doors, pushed them open, lost interest in what lay behind.

"Pretty dull," he said, and leaned forward, ready for the jump. "Okay. Let's say Life Is."

"Are you sure?"

"I'm ready to try . . ."

"Remember the door says *Life Is*," I said. "It is not kidding. Invisible letters underneath, if you want: *No Matter What Seems to Be.*

"Life Is."

"HA, DICKIE!" I shouted in Samurai, curved sword glittering in my hand. "THERE IN ITS COFFIN LIES THE BODY OF YOUR BROTHER! IS THERE NO DEATH?"

"Life Is," he said, trusting, "No Matter What."

I slipped into a black robe, disappeared my head way back inside its hood, stood on tiptoe, spoke ominous and hollow. "I am Death, little child, and I shall come for you in my time, and nothing there be that can stay my call . . ." I can be pretty ominous; had myself a little worried in there.

Still he clung to the truth he tested. "Life Is," he said. "No Matter What."

"Hey, guy," I said, changed into my yellow plaid sportcoat. "It's no big thing. You don't expect your shoes to last forever, do you, or your car, or your life? Common sense . . . everything wears out!"

"Life Is," he said. "No Matter What."

Then, disguised as myself, I said, "Appearances change."

"Life Is," he replied.

"It's easy to say that when you're well and happy, Captain," I said. "What do you say when you're bleeding, or you're sick, or you're depressed your girlfriend left you, your wife doesn't understand who you are, you've lost your job and you're broke, looking at the bottom as low as you can go?"

"Life Is."

"Does Life care about appearances?"

He thought for a moment. Any question could be a trick question. "No."

"Does Life know about appearances?"

Long silence. "Give me a hint."

"Does light know about darkness?" I asked.

"No!"

"If Life Is, does It know only Itself?"

"Yes?"

"No guessing."

"YES!"

"Does it know the stars?"

". . . no."

"Does it know beginning and ending," I said, "space and time?"

"Life Is. Always and forever. No."

Why are simple things so difficult? I thought. Is means

Is. Not Was or Will Be or Used to Be or May Not Have Been or Could Flame Out Tomorrow. *Is*.

"Does Life know Dickie Bach?"

Long silence. "It doesn't know my body."

There you go, I thought. "Does It know your . . . street address?"

He laughed. "No!"

"Does It know your . . . planet?"

"No."

"Does It know your . . . name?"

"No."

Pop quiz. "Does Life know you?"

"It knows . . . my life," he said. "It knows my spirit."

"Are you sure?"

"I don't care what you say. Life knows my life."

"Can your body be destroyed?" I asked.

"Of course it can, Richard."

"Can your life be destroyed?"

"Never!" he said, surprised.

"Oh, come on, Dickie. Are you saying you can't be killed?"

"Two kinds of killed. Anybody can kill the appearance of me. Nobody can take my life away." He thought for a second. "Not if Life Is."

"So," I said.

"So?" he said. "What?"

"Lesson's over. You just brought God to Life."

"An all-powerful God?" he asked.

"Is Life all-powerful?" I said.

"In its world. In the Real world, Life Is. Nothing destroys Life."

"In the world of Appearances?"

"Appearances are appearances," he said. "Nothing destroys Life."

"Does Life love you?"

"Life knows me. I'm undestroyable. And I'm a nice person . . ."

"What if you're not? If Life doesn't see appearances, if Life isn't aware of space and time, if Life sees only Life, if Life doesn't know Conditions, can Life see you as a good person or a bad person?"

"Life sees me perfect?"

"What do you think?" I said. "Do you call that love? I'm open for suggestions."

He was quiet for a long time, narrowed his eyes, cocked his head.

"What's wrong?" I said.

For a moment he looked at me as if he held a detonator in his hand, my beautiful structure took a lifetime for me to learn and he hated to blow it all apart. But I was not his only future, he had his own life stretching ahead, and one cannot live ideas that one cannot trust.

"Tell me," I said, heart beating faster.

"Don't get me wrong," he said. "I have to admit, the

way you lay it out, logically your religion may be true." He thought for a moment. "But . . ."

"But . . . ?"

"But what's it got to do with my life as an Apparent Human Being here on the Appearance of Earth? Your Is is nice, Richard," he said, "but *so what*?"

Twenty-six

I laughed at myself in the quiet. How many thousands of times has it happened to me, that it suddenly matters what someone else thinks, or what someone else might decide to do? As though a seam has gently parted below the waterline of my inner ship, a worried tension floods me and I drag lower in the sea, not so light and fast and easy to turn as I like to be and not knowing why.

"Haven't you ever thought So What?" said Dickie. "You must have!"

I bent down low, threw hard, shied the stone off the hillside. With enough thrust, I thought, nearly anything can fly.

"You sent Shepherd," I said, "because you wanted to learn what I know."

"I didn't send Shepherd . . ."

I picked another stone, continued my silent research in rock aerodynamics.

"Yes," he said. "I had to learn what you know. I still do. I'm sorry if I hurt your feelings with So What."

I had chosen silence to keep from forcing him to my way of thinking . . . he had heard silence as hurt feelings over a fair question. How hard it is for people to understand each other unless they already agree!

"Help me with this problem," I said. "I want to show you what I've learned. I want to give it to you free, because you're going to do something different with that learning than I've done and somehow you're going to find a way to tell me what you did with it different, and why. I want that to happen. Do you believe me?"

He nodded.

"But something else I know is Never Convince Anybody. When you said So What I saw this pink neon sign: Sell Him, Prove Your Truth or He Won't Believe What You're Saying!"

"No," he said. "That's not what . . ."

"I don't mind telling you, I don't mind explaining as

clearly as I know how, but remember I can't take responsibility for someone over whom I have no authority . . . for anyone, that is, but me."

"But I . . ."

"Leaning on other people for understanding is like leaning on doctors for healing, Dickie. We can only benefit when they're available and when they're right . . . when they're gone or wrong we're out of luck. But if instead we spend a lifetime learning how to understand what we know, then that inner knowing self is always with us, and when it's wrong we can change it till it works every time, almost."

"Richard, I . . ."

"Remember, Captain: The reason I'm here is not to convince you, or to convert you, or to make you into me. I have a hard enough time making Richard into me. I'm nobody's leader but my own. I would frankly feel better if you stopped caring who I am and what I believe and why I'm different from all your other futures. I owe you information, and an answer to your curiosity. I do not owe you a conversion to my way of thinking which may all be lies."

In exchange for my sermon he traded me a long silence. Fair trade, I thought, and didn't speak.

He sighed. "I understand that you are not my leader,"

he said, "and that you do not take responsibility for any-thing that I may or may not do for the rest of my natural life or lives throughout all eternity. I agree to hold you harmless for any injury real or imagined which might result from any word of yours which I might rightly or wrongly apply or misapply in any situation in any future or alternate future I may choose. Do you understand?"

I shook my head.

"What do you mean, no? Can't you get it? YOU ARE NOT MY LEADER OR MY GUIDE OR MY TEACHER, NO MATTER HOW MANY . . ."

"No good," I said. "I want it in writing."

His face was a wonder to behold. "You WHAT? I'm telling you that I understand you don't want to be any-body's leader and you're telling me that's not good enough for . . ."

I handed him a fine smooth rock to throw. "Just kid-ding," I said. "Just fluffin' you, Dickie. I want to be sure you understand. I don't need any agreement in writing."

He studied the rock in his hand: didn't throw it, didn't drop it. "Okay," he said at last. "About Life Is. So what?"

"What do you know about arithmetic?" I said.

"What does any fourth-grader know about arithmetic?" he said, knowing I had to be going somewhere, hoping I wasn't fluffing him again. "I know the same as everybody else."

"That's good enough," I said. "I think that Life is expressed in Appearance the same way that numbers are expressed in spacetime. Let's take the number nine. Or would you rather use another number?"

"Eight," he said, in case nine was a trick number.

"Okay, let's take the number eight. We can print an eight in ink on paper, we can cast eight in bronze, we can chip eight into stone, arrange eight dandelions in a row, stack eight dodecahedrons carefully one on top of the other. How many different ways can we express the idea eight?"

He shrugged. "Zillions of ways. No end of ways."

"But wait," I said. "See this torch, and this sledge-hammer? We can also burn the page, melt the bronze, turn stone to dust, blow dandelions to the wind, crush dodecahedrons to a splintered mass."

"I get it. We can destroy numbers."

"No. We can destroy the *appearance* of numbers in spacetime. We can create appearances, we can destroy appearances."

He nodded.

"But before time began, Dickie, and right this minute, and after time and space have washed away, the reality of the idea eight stands, indestructible by appearances. When the Big Bang has turned to the Big Crunch and all matter is crushed to a particle so small that it no longer exists, the idea eight floats serene, perfect and absolutely uncaring."

"It doesn't care?"

"Now, here's an axe," I said. "Chop up the idea of the number eight so it no longer exists. Take as long as you want. Tell me when you're done."

He laughed. "I can't chop ideas, Richard!"

"I couldn't either."

"So my body," he said, "is no more the real me than a written-down number is the real number."

I nodded. "But I'm getting there a lot slower than you are. Wait up."

He waited.

"What other number is like the number eight?" I asked, wondering for a second if I cared whether he believed in my pictures. I don't care whether he believes, I thought. I care whether he understands.

"Seven?"

"How many eights are there in arithmetic?"

He thought for seconds. "One."

"That's what I think, too. The idea of any number is unique, there is no other idea like it in existence. The entire Principle of Numbers depends upon dear eight, and without eight the whole Principle would collapse."

"Oh, come on, now . . ."

"Don't think so? Let's say we've managed to destroy the number eight. Quick: What's four plus four? Six plus two? Ten minus two?"

"Oh," he said.

"You've got it, then. An indefinite number of numbers, each number different from all the others, each as important to the Principle as the Principle is important to every one."

"The Principle needs every number!" he said. "I never thought of that."

"You will," I said. "Real, indestructible, life beyond appearances—yet any number can be expressed simultaneously in any of the infinite worlds-of-appearance that it wishes."

"How do we change?" he asked. "Where does belief come from? How do we all of a sudden forget everything that's true and turn into speechless babies overnight?"

I bit my lip. "I don't know."

"What? You've got this whole puzzle worked out and there's a piece missing?"

"I know we're free to believe any kind of lifetime," I said. "I know we do it for the fun of learning and the power of remembering who we are. How do we forget? *Welcome to spacetime, check your memory at the door?* Something happens, but I haven't found what it is that wipes us out when we make the jump."

He smiled at my puzzlement, an odd smile I couldn't fathom, and after a moment he nodded. "I can get along with a piece missing," he said. "Something Happens. We forget. Go on."

"Anyway, once we're in spacetime," I said, "we're free

to believe that we exist alone and unconnected, we're free to say the Principle of Numbers is nonsense."

He nodded, putting that together.

"The Principle doesn't notice spacetime," I said, "because spacetime isn't. So the Principle doesn't hear anguished prayer or wicked curse, there's no such thing as sacrilege or heresy or blasphemy or impiety or irreverence or abomination. The Principle builds no temples, hires no missionaries, fights no wars. It is heedless, utterly unaware when symbols of its numbers are nailed to crosses, hacked to pieces by other symbols and burned to ash."

"It doesn't care," he said, reluctant.

"Does Mom care about you?" I asked.

"She loves me!"

"Did she know or did she care, last time you played cops and robbers, that you were shot dead ten times an hour?"

"Hm."

"Same with the Principle," I said. "It doesn't notice the games that matter so much to us. Try it now. Turn so that your back is to the Infinite Principle of Numbers, to the Immortal Reality of Numerical Being."

He shifted on the hilltop, turned a little left.

"Speak out: *I hate the Principle of Numbers!*"

"I hate the Principle of Numbers," he said, not much conviction.

"Try this," I said. *"The creepy dumb Principle of Numbers eats refined sugar, saturated oils and red meat!"*

He laughed.

"Careful on this one, Captain. We're going to need a lot of courage to shout this one, since if we're wrong here we can get fried: *THE ROTTEN LYING LOUSY NO-GOOD SAND-WORM USELESS SO-CALLED PRINCIPLE OF NUMBERS IS DUMBER THAN HORSE-FLIES! IT COULDN'T HIT US WITH A LIGHTNING BOLT TO PROVE ITS CRUMMY SELF EXISTS IF IT TRIED!"*

He got lost after sand-worm and made up the rest, but finished a fiery enough curse against the Principle that we would have been toast if it cared.

Nothing happened.

"So we can ignore the Principle, we can hate it, curse it, crusade against it," I said, "we can make fun of it. No wrath from heaven, nor the faintest frown on high. Why not?"

He considered that for a long time.

"Why doesn't the Principle of Numbers care?" I asked.

"Because it isn't listening," he said at last.

"So there's no penalty when we trash the Principle?"

"No penalty," he said.

"Wrong."

"What? It's not listening!"

"It's not listening, Dickie," I said, "but *we are*! When we turn our back on the Principle of Numbers, what happens in our arithmetic?"

"Nothing adds up?"

"Nothing. Answers come out different every time, business and science dissolve in tangles. Abandon Principle, and it's not the Principle that suffers, it's us!"

"Holy cow," he said.

"But remember Principle, and that instant everything

works again. No apology required, It couldn't hear one if we shouted. Nobody's on probation, nobody's punished, no scoldings from the Infinite One. Remembering brings sudden healing through all our sums, for even in the imaginary playgrounds of appearance, the Principle is real."

"Interesting," he said, not believing but following.

"And now I've caught up with you, Dickie. Now let's say instead of the Principle of Numbers, the Principle of Life."

"Life Is," he said.

"Pure life, pure love, knowing its own pure self. Let's say that each of us is a perfect unique expression of that Principle, that we exist beyond spacetime, that we are immortal, eternal, indestructible."

"Let's say. So what?"

"So we're free to do anything we want except two things: we can't create reality and we can't destroy it."

"What can we do?"

"Marvelous Nothing, in all its diamond forms. When we walk into Lease-A-Life, what do we expect to rent? We can check out unlimited worlds of appearance, we can buy births and deaths, we can shop for tragedy and delight and

190

disaster and peace and terror and nobility and cruelty and
heaven and hell, we can take home our beliefs, savor them
in excruciating searing joyful delicious microscopic detail.
But before time and after, through every moment, Life Is,
and We Are. The one thing we fear most is the one thing
that is not possible: we cannot die, we cannot be destroyed.
Life Is. We Are."

"We Are," he said, unimpressed. "So What?"

"You tell me, Dickie. What's the difference between
victims of circumstance, trapped in lives they didn't ask for,
and masters of choice, leading lives they can change at
will?"

"Victims are helpless," he said. "Masters aren't."

I nodded. "That's so what."

Twenty-seven

*H*e had given me the chance to say what I wanted to say, he was thinking about it, and I figured I'd best be on my way for a while.

I looked across the landscape, wondered how it would look when I saw it again. "See you next time," I whispered.

"Are you a master?" he asked.

"Of course I am! Me and you and everybody else. But we forget."

"How do they do it?" he said.

"How does who do what?"

"How do masters change their lives at will?"

I smiled at the question. "Power tools."

"Pardon?"

"Another difference between masters and victims is that victims haven't learned power tools and masters use 'em all the time."

"Electric drills? Buzz saws?" He was adrift, asking for help. A good teacher would have left him alone to puzzle it out, but I'm too chatty to teach.

"Not buzz saws. *Choice.* The enchanted blade, with an edge that shapes lifetimes. Yet if we're afraid to choose anything but what we've got, what good is choice? Might as well leave choice wrapped up in its box, don't bother to read the instructions."

"Who's afraid to use it?" he said. "What's scary about choice?"

"It makes us different!"

"Oh, come on . . ."

"Okay, don't choose," I said. "Do what everyone else would do, every minute of your life. What happens?"

"I go to school."

193

"Yes. And?"

"I graduate."

"Yes. And?"

"I get a job."

"Yes. And?"

"I get married."

"Yes. And?"

"I have children."

"Yes. And?"

"I help them through school."

"Yes. And?"

"I retire."

"Yes. And?"

"I die."

"And when you die, listen to your last words."

He thought about those. *"So what."*

"Even though you do everything that everyone expects you to do: you're a law-abiding citizen, you're the perfect husband and father, you vote, you give to charity, you're kind to animals. You live what they expect and you die from *so what?*"

"Hm."

"Because you never chose your life, Dickie! You never asked for change, you never asked what you loved and you never found it, you never hurled yourself into the world that mattered most to you, never fought dragons that you thought could eat you up, never inched yourself out on cliffsides clinging by the tips of your skill a thousand feet over destruction because your life was there and you had to bring it home from terror! Choice, Dickie! Choose what you love and chase it at top speed and I your future do solemnly promise that you will never die from *so what!*"

He looked at me sideways. "Are you trying to convince me?"

"I'm trying," I said, "to turn you astray from Going Along. I owe that to you."

"What if I do it? What happens if I learn choosing for myself, no matter what other people say, and I go out there on the cliffs. Will your magic blade keep me safe?"

I sighed. "Dickie, when did safety become your ambition? Running from safety is the only way to make your last word *Yes!*"

"The sycamore tree," he said.

"Excuse me?"

". . . in the front yard. It's always there, it's always safe. When I'm scared I'd give anything to be that tree. When I'm not I couldn't stand the dull life."

The tree lives there yet, I thought, bigger than he'd know it, leafier, lasted another half century by digging its feet ever deeper in the dirt.

"Run from safety doesn't mean destroy yourself," I said. "You don't strap on a racing plane until you learn to fly a Cub first. Little choices, little adventures before big ones. But one day comes the middle of an air race, in the wide-open blast-furnace roar of this monster engine, the world's a steep green blur fifty feet down, you're pulling six G's around the pylons and all at once you remember: I chose this minute to happen to me! I built this life! I wanted it more than anything else, I crawled and walked and ran to get it and now it's *here!*"

"I don't know," he said. "Do I have to risk my life?"

"Of course you do! With every choice you risk the life

you would have had; with every decision, you lose it. Sure, an alternate Dickie in an alternate world splits away and lives what you might have chosen, but that's his choice, not yours. In school and business and marriage, in any adventure you pick, if you care what your last words will be, you trust what you know and you dare toward your hope."

"And if I'm wrong," he said, "I die."

"If you want security," I said, "you've come to the wrong arena. The only security is *Life Is,* and that's all that matters. Absolute, unchanging, perfect. But Security in Appearances? Even the sycamore falls to dust, someday."

He gritted his teeth, his face a panic of worry-lines.

I laughed at the look. "The wood disintegrates, the symbol vanishes, not the spirit of its life. The belief of your body shatters, not the believer who shaped it."

"Maybe my spirit loves change," he said. "My body hates it."

I remembered. Safe and warm, under the covers, six-thirty sound asleep in the winter morning, and BOBBY! DICKIE! RISE AND SHINE! READY FOR SCHOOL! and I'd struggle awake, swear that if I ever grew up I would never get out of bed before noon. Same in the Air Force: alert siren goes off, wired to my pillow at two in the morning HONGA-HONGA-HONGA! and I am somehow

supposed to wake up? and fly? an airplane? *in the dark?*
Body: Not possible! Spirit: Do it! Now!

"Body hates change." I nodded. "But look at your body
. . . every day a little taller, a little changed; Dickie melts
upward into Richard, doomed to adulthood! No body's
destroyed more completely than a child's grown up, Captain. Gone without a trace, no coffin, not even ashes left to
mourn."

"Help," he said. "I need all the power tools I can get!"

"They're already in your hands. What can you say to any
appearance?"

"Life Is."

"And?"

"And what?" he said.

I hinted. "Choice."

"And I can change appearances."

"Within certain limits?"

"Limits, heck!" he said. "I don't have to breathe, if I
don't want to breathe! Where are your limits now?"

198

I shrugged.

"When masters don't like the way things seem to be, Richard, why don't they just stop breathing? Why don't they just quit the world of Appearances when they run into a really hard problem, and go home?"

"Why quit when we can change the world? Declare Life Is, right in the face of appearance, draw enchanted Choice, and after a decent work-filled interval, the world changes."

"Always?"

"Usually."

The air went out of him. "Usually? You give me a magic formula and your guarantee is it usually works?"

"When it doesn't, the Principle of Coincidence shows up."

"The principle of coincidence," he said.

"You've chosen some life-affirming change in your immediate world of Appearance, let's say. You decide changes will appear."

He nodded.

"You declare *Life Is,* knowing it's true, and you work your little heart out to transform what you will."

He nodded.

"And it doesn't change," I said.

"I was going to ask."

"Here's what you do: You keep working, and you watch for coincidence to come strolling your way. Watch carefully, for it always comes in disguise."

He nodded.

"And you follow that coincidence!"

Dickie was unmoved. "An example would help," he said.

An example. "We need to walk through this brick wall, because it locks us into an appearance of life that we choose to change."

He nodded.

"We work like crazy to change it, but our wall remains brick, and it gets if anything harder than ever. We've checked: there's no secret door, no ladder, no shovel to dig under . . . solid brick."

He agreed. "Solid brick."

"Then be still and listen. Is that a faint muffled chugging behind us? Has yon bulldozer operator left an engine running during her lunch break and the machine slipped into double compound low gear? Is the machine coincidentally rumbling toward our wall?"

"I'm supposed to trust in coincidence?"

"Remember that this world is not reality. It's a playground of appearances on which we practice overcoming seems-to-be with our knowing of Is. The Principle of Coincidence is a power tool that promises, in this playground, to take us to the other side of our wall."

"What did the principle of coincidence ever do for you?"

"What hasn't it done? Every major turn of my life pivoted on some coincidence."

"Oh . . ." he scoffed. "Tell me one."

"You remember riding your bike to the airport, do you remember clutching your fingers through the chain-link and hanging on the fence by the *Pilots and Passengers Only Beyond This Point* sign?"

He nodded. "Lots of times."

"And wishing you could fly, and drawing pictures of airplanes and building airplane models and writing about airplanes in class and telling yourself that someday you'll be a pilot?"

He opened his eyes wide. The old guy remembers.

"Flying was a brick wall," I said. "When I wanted to learn, nothing happened. No money for flying lessons, no friends with airplanes, no sudden fairy godmothers, no gifts from family. Dad hated airplanes. I finished high school and enrolled in college. Classes in chemistry and analytic geometry and composition and ichthyology and the one that changed my life: the class in archery."

"Bows and arrows?"

"Everybody had to take a course in physical education. Archery was the easiest way around it."

He nodded.

"Came Monday morning, I was one in a class of twenty lined side by side outdoors. Next to me by coincidence was a senior, getting the last of his credits for graduation. We both stood resolute, firing arrows at our hay bales, when by coincidence a lightplane flew overhead on its way to Long Beach Municipal Airport. Instead of firing his next arrow, Bob Keech relaxed his bow and he looked up at that airplane. One look, and he changed my life."

"By looking up?"

"Nobody in Long Beach looks at airplanes, as common over the city as sparrows over housetops. This fellow, I thought, bothering to lift his head to watch a plane, must somehow care. Lightning destiny, I spoke before I knew it couldn't be: 'Bob? I'll bet you're a flight instructor and you're looking for someone to wash and polish your airplane and if they do that for you, you'll teach them to fly.'"

"He said yes," Dickie guessed.

"No. He looked surprised and he said, *How did you know?*"

"Oh, come on," said Dickie, not believing. "How could that happen? There's no reason that could happen."

"There was a reason, all right. Bob Keech had just earned his Limited Flight Instructor's certificate, and he needed to teach five students before he could become a real, permanent Certified Flight Instructor. That was the reason."

"But how did you know he needed to teach somebody to fly?"

"Intuition? Hope? Luck, I thought then. In six months, Bob Keech taught me to fly. I ran away from school to join the Air Force and the rest of my life angled up into the air. The Principle of Coincidence had arranged my destiny, but I didn't know it existed till twenty years later."

"How does it work?"

"Like attracts like. It'll surprise you as long as you live. Choose a love and work to make it true, and somehow something will happen, something you couldn't plan, will come along to move like to like, to set you loose, to set you on the way to your next brick wall."

"My next wall! *Next* wall?"

"It's not as hard as it sounds. We don't have to work to put ourselves into the worst possible situation we can imagine . . . whenever we forget our magic, that happens by itself. But the fun's not getting into trouble, it's getting out. The game is to remember who we are, and use our power tools. How can we learn unless we practice?"

He was doubtful. "I don't know . . ."

Does he want a trouble-free future? I thought. Why pick spacetime if he doesn't want trouble? "Thought experiment," I said. "Imagine there's nothing you want to change in your world. It couldn't possibly be any better than it already is."

He thought for a moment. "Hurray!" he said. "This feels great!"

"Okay," I said. "Now stay in that world for a month. Two months. A year. Two years. Three. How does it feel?"

"I want to learn something new. I want to do something different."

"And there you have the reason for the world of appearances."

"We like learning new things?"

"We like remembering what we already know. When you hear your favorite music, or watch a good movie over again, or read your favorite story, you know what it's going to sound like, don't you, what it's going to look like, how it's going to turn out? The fun comes from living it over again, as many times as you want. Same with our powers. First we dimly remember, and timid, we try Choice; the Principle of Coincidence; Whatever We Hold in Thought Comes True in Our Experience; Like Attracts Like; we experiment with the Law of Changing Appearances, to make our outer world reflect our inner."

"Scary."

"And when it changes once, three times, ten, we grow a little bolder and sure enough, the tools *work*! With practice we trust them utterly, we've remembered all they have to show us, we can change appearances however we wish, and we move on to new adventures, with different laws."

"Tell me more tools," he said.

"How many do you need? Our hearts are full of cosmic laws. Learn just a few, get good at those, there's nothing can stand between you and the person you want to be."

"But that's why I'm talking to you! I'm not sure who it is I want to be!"

I frowned then, in the silence, at a puzzle I couldn't solve. "That," I said, "can stand between you."

Twenty-eight

*I*t must happen to us all, I thought. We pack up what we've learned so far and leave the familiar behind. No fun, that shearing separation, but somewhere within we must dimly know that saying good-bye to safety brings the only security we'll ever know.

How many times does it happen in our lives, hundreds?

We run from the safety of family to the strangers of the playground. Run from the safety of friends next door into the cauldron of school. From the safety of listening, in class, to the terror of delivering our own oral report. From the peaceful stillness of the high-dive platform to the whirling test of a two-and-a-half gainer. From the simple ease of English into the umlaut deeps of German. From the warmth of dependence into the ice of on-our-own. From the cocoon of training into the whirlwind of business. From the shelter of the ground into the lovely hazards of flight. From the certainty of singledom to the stormy faith of marriage. From the worn-jacket comfort of living into the ominous adventure of dying. Every step in every proud life is a run from safety to the dark, and the only thing to trust is what we think is true.

How do I know this, I wondered, where did I learn?

No wait for sleep, no Dickie to fetch my answers, a moment after I wondered, I knew.

Twenty-nine

*B*efore ever I realized that home is the known and loved I felt it, a magnet sunk beneath words. When I left the Air Force, the closest place that felt like home was Long Beach, California.

There I moved, and not far out of town found a position as technical writer in the Publications Division of the Douglas Aircraft Company. Writing pilots' handbooks for the DC-8 jet transport and the C-124 cargo plane was a way to survive with a typewriter and with airplanes. What better job than this?

The Publications Division building was called A-23, acres under one high roof, a giant steel island rising abruptly from a sea of parking lots rimmed by miles of chain-link fence.

Enter those doors, stamp my time-card, turn, and a vast

plain of engineer's drafting tables stretched to the horizon, a shifting monocolor tapestry of white shirts dyed tea-green by fluorescent lights high overhead.

From the drafting tables came the drawings for airplane handbooks; the words were up to us. Take a design engineer's careful explanation of what happens when all throttles are advanced, for instance, figure out what she means and say it so that a pilot can read and understand.

Pilots have an eighth-grade comprehension, we were told, but don't force them to use it. Not many syllables. Short sentences. Instructions clearly written.

The Go-Around checklist for the C-124, for example. It had been written in the pilot's handbook that should the aircraft commander change his mind about landing and decide instead to climb back into the sky, he was to call, "Takeoff Power!" to the flight engineer, who would then push all throttles to full power, same as for takeoff.

In a moment or two, after the aircraft showed a positive rate of climb, the pilot would call, "Landing Gear Up," and the co-pilot would lift the landing gear lever, which would raise the wheels to let the airplane climb faster yet.

It happened one day that a C-124 had descended a little too low on its final approach to land and the pilot decided to go around and try again.

"Takeoff Power!" he called, as our book instructed. The flight engineer, ready to land, thought the airplane was within an inch of the runway. When he heard "Take Off Power!" he took it off . . . he cut the throttles of all four engines back to idle.

So, one of the largest airplanes in the world fell thus out of the sky, touched down half a mile from the airport and slid for most of the next minute through rice paddies, shedding parts, till its dented nose rested on the first few inches of the runway.

A tart note from the United States Air Force reached the director of the Douglas Aircraft Publications Division at A-23. Hastily we changed the C-124 checklist command from "Takeoff Power" to "Maximum Power" and all resolved to think carefully about the consequence of every word we chose. An important job, technical writing.

Most of us handbook writers at Douglas were former military pilots, latter-day scribes rewriting the Bible. We could speak directly to the designer, translate meanings into simple words by which we all could live. Not only a responsible job, but a useful and rewarding lifework.

After a few months, though, I turned restive. From time to time, supervisors disagreed with my syntax, decided that they knew better than I, where a comma, might belong.

"Settle down, Richard, settle down," said my colleagues

211

from their typewriters. "It's only a comma, we are not writing the Great American Handbook here. Douglas pays good money and you'll never lose your job. Count your blessings and don't comment, please, on the supervisor's punctuation."

I had a hard time accepting. Why was this dry straw under my feet, when there was fresh sweet clover green just past yonder fence? If I were writing on my own, there'd be no one to stab me with commas. Commas, would, go, exactly, where, I, darn, well wa,nted t,h,e,m to go,!

Slow dawning of an old dilemma: I had the heart of a prima donna and the body of an ox.

"I'm leaving Douglas Aircraft," I said at lunch hour, perched on the front fender of my third-hand Borgward. "I'm going freelance for a while, I've got some stories that aren't going to get printed in Technical Order 1-C-124G-1 no matter where I put my commas."

"Sure," said Bill Coffin, crunching a potato chip alongside. "We're all leaving Douglas Aircraft. Zack's going to get called by United Airlines next month and he'll be captain in a year; Willy Pearson's patent is coming in on his automatic well-logger and he'll be a rich man; Martha Dyer's novel is off in the mail again and this time it's sold for sure and a best-seller." He stirred his lunch bag. "I've got too many of these things. Want a potato chip?"

"Thanks."

"I think there's money to be made in commercial fishing, as you may be tired of hearing. But you notice, Richard, that none of us has quite nipped over the fence yet. Douglas may not be as glamorous as, say, heading out to sea in a 48-foot trawler, but Douglas is what we call secure, do you know?"

I nodded.

"Do you know what I mean, secure? This is not the world's hardest job, and as long as nobody's listening between you and me we're getting paid more for less work than anybody we know and as long as America needs airliners and the Air Force needs cargo planes me and you are never gonna get fired."

"Yeah . . ." I nibbled the edge of the potato chip, more courtesy than hunger.

"You believe me, but you still want to fly the coop, don't you?"

I didn't answer.

"Do you really think you can make this kind of money writing freelance? How many stories would you have to sell to match what you're getting paid right now?"

"A lot," I said.

He shrugged. "You write your stories for the fun of it, you work at Douglas for the money, and if the stories don't sell at least you aren't starving to death. And if they do sell, you can quit."

The siren sounded, end of lunch hour, and Bill scattered the rest of his chips on the ground, a mariner's treat for the seagulls.

"You're still a kid and you're not listening and you're gonna quit," he said. "But some day you'll wish to God you were right back here at A-23 and glad for supervisors telling you where to put your commas." He pointed across the parking lot. "Look there. I've got a dime in my pocket says the day is gonna come that you'll stand at that gate, outside lookin' in, and remember what security means."

No! I thought. Don't tell me that my security comes from somebody else! Tell me *I'm* responsible. Tell me security is a by-product of the gift I give of my skill and my learning and my love into the world. Tell me security comes from an idea given time and care. I claim this for my truth, no matter how many stable solid paychecks might come from the Accounting Department of Douglas Aircraft. Dear God, I thought, don't give me a job, give me *ideas,* and let me take it from there!

I laughed, brushed crumbs, hopped off the fender.

"Maybe you're right, Willy. Time's gonna come. I'm gonna stand at that gate, outside lookin' in."

The next day I gave my notice, and by the end of the month I was a freelance writer on my way to hungry.

✦

Twenty years later, not to the day but close, visiting Los Angeles, I drove south on the San Diego Freeway, saw a familiar sign, turned on impulse north up Hawthorne Boulevard, snaked a little east.

How the body remembers the drive to work! Turn left here, now left again, up this long avenue lined in eucalyptus.

It was nearly noon, bright sunlight when I found the place, and sure enough, there stretched the same diamond-wire fence around the same ocean-wide parking lot, the same steel building jutting straight up, bigger than I remembered. I stopped at the gate, got out of the car, heart beating fast, the scene burning into my eyes.

The parking lot was faded gray pavement, weeds growing through cracks, not one car in three thousand spaces.

There were chains around the gateposts, chains snapped tight with massive padlocks.

Times are hard for freelance writers, I remembered, but times get hard for big airplane companies, too.

Way off in that lot shimmered a ghostly Bill Coffin, betting the man I used to be, and just now he won his bet. I remembered what that meant, *security,* and I stood alone, locked out, staring through the gate into nothing.

I tossed a dime through the chains to my friend and after a long quiet time I drove away, wondering, where, he, was.

Thirty

$\mathcal{T}$he world's going to pieces in wars and terrorism," said the commentator, the moment the screen crackled alive. "Tonight, we're sorry to report, there's death and starvation and drought and flood and pestilence and epidemics and unemployment worldwide, the sea is dying and the future with it, the climate's changing the forests are burning and hatred runs amok, haves versus nots and single-issues versus let-it-be's, recessions and ozone holes and greenhouse effects and chlorofluorocarbons, species going excuse me gone extinct, drugs run wild and education's dead and cities crumbling and everywhere's overcrowded and crime owns the streets and whole countries are running bankrupt and there's pollution for air and radiation for soil, there's acid rain and crops failing, fires and mudslides and volcanoes and earthquakes and hurricanes and tidal waves and tornadoes and floods and oil spills and nuclear meltdowns all foretold, some say, in the Book of Look Out and by the way there's a monster asteroid tumbling toward the earth if it so much as nicks the pole it will wipe out all life on the planet."

"Want another channel?" I asked.

"This one's fine," said Leslie.

Dickie cringed behind my eyes. "We're all going to die."

"Some say." I watched Armageddon on the screen.

"Aren't you ever down?" he said. "Don't you ever feel bad? Don't you get depressed?"

"Will that help? Why should I be depressed?"

"What you're watching! What you're hearing! They're talking about the End of the World! Are they kidding?"

"No," I told him. "Things are a lot worse than they can say in thirty minutes."

"Then there's no hope! What are you doing here?"

"No hope? Of course there's no hope, Captain! There's no hope that the way things were yesterday is the way they're going to stay tomorrow. There's no hope that anything but reality lasts, and reality isn't place and time. We call this place Earth, but its real name is Change. People

218

who need hope either don't pick Earth or they don't take the games here all that seriously." I felt like a seasoned planet-rider, telling him, then realized that I was.

"But the news is awful!"

"It's like flying, Dickie. Sometimes we'll go out to fly and the weather-mavens say look out for thunderstorms and ice and freezing rain, careful for the sandstorms and mountaintops obscured in fog, there's wind-shear and microbursts and the lifted index is off the clock you're a fool to dare take off today. And we go out and fly and it's a nice flight."

"A nice flight?"

"The news is like the weather. We don't fly through the forecast, we fly through the weather that's there when we are."

"And the weather that's there is always nice?"

"Nope. Sometimes it's terrible. Sometimes it's worse than they say."

"So what do you do?"

"I handle the sky that's around me at the moment in the best way I know how. I'm not responsible for surviving all the weather everywhere, I'm just responsible for getting through the weather I find in a block from one wingtip to the other and from the bottom of the wheels to the top of the rudders. I'm responsible because that's the weather I draw by choosing my time to fly and deciding where I point Daisy's nose. So far, I haven't been killed."

"And the world?" There was concern in his eyes, he needed to know.

"The world's not a sphere, Dickie, it's a big floating pyramid. At the bottom of the pyramid is the lowest life-form you can imagine, hateful, vicious, destroying for destruction's sake, devoid of empathy, one step above consciousness so savage it self-destructs the instant it's born. There's room for that kind of consciousness, lots of room, right here on our triangular third planet."

"What's at the top of the pyramid?"

"At the top is consciousness so refined it barely recognizes anything but light. Beings who live for their loves, for their highest right, creatures of perfect perspective, who die with a loving smile upon whatever monster would strike them down for the fun of watching someone die. Whales are like that, I think. Most dolphins. Some people —the human beings among us."

"In between are the rest of us," he said.

"You and me, kid."

"Can't we change the world?"

"Absolutely," I said. "We can change our world any way we want."

"Not our world. The world. Can't we make it better?"

"Better for me and you," I said, "is not better for every-body."

"Peace is better than war."

"The ones near the top of the pyramid would probably agree. Peace would make them happier."

"And the ones near the bottom . . ."

". . . love battle! There's always a reason to fight. With luck it's a burning cause: this war we fight for God, this war's to save the Homeland, this one to cleanse the Race, to expand the Empire, to get the tin and tungsten. We fight because the pay's good, because it's more exciting destroying lives than building them, because war beats work for a living, because everybody else is fighting, be-cause it'll show I'm a man, because I like to kill."

"Terrible," he said.

"Not terrible," I said. "Predictable. When one planet

makes room for so wide a spectrum of mind, we expect a lot of conflict. Is that okay with you?"

He frowned. "No."

"Next time pick a narrow planet."

"What if there is no next-time?" he said. "What if you're wrong about other lives than this?"

"Doesn't make any difference," I said. "We build our personal world calm or wild according to what we want to live. We can weave utter peace in the midst of chaos. We can destroy in the midst of paradise. Depends on how we shape our spirit."

"Richard," he said, "everything you think is so personal! Can't you imagine that there may be some things over which you have no control? That there may be some completely different scheme—that life just happened, for no reason, no matter what you think or don't think, or the whole planet's an experiment by saucer-people watching in a microscope?"

"Too dull, Captain, no control. Too boring. When I go along for the ride, I feel useless, I'm discontent. It's no fun flying when I can't steer the plane; I'd rather bail out and walk. So long as the saucer-people stay cool and cunning, so long as they let me think I'm master of my own little fate, I'll play their game. But the minute they pull my strings, I cut 'em."

"Maybe they're pulling your strings v-e-r-y c-a-r-e-f-u-l-l-y," he said.

I smiled at him. "So far they haven't made a slip. The minute I feel strings, the minute I see threads on my wrists, out come the scissors."

At the end of the documented disaster, the commentator wished us a happy day, and hoped to see us tomorrow.

Leslie turned to me. "Dickie's there, isn't he?"

"How can you tell?"

"He's worried about the future."

She's psychic, I thought. "Have you two been talking?"

"No," she said. "If he weren't worried, after what we just saw, I'd think you were losing your mind."

Thirty-one

*L*eslie was humming to her computer the next morning as I stopped at the office door.

I knocked on the doorjamb. "Just me."

"Not just you," she said, looking up. "You are a lot! You are my darling!" Whatever she was working on, it was going well. When it's not going well, she doesn't hum, she doesn't look up, she just opens an extra track of consciousness for me and carries on with all the rest at once.

"How much do you weigh?" I said.

She raised her hands over her head. "Look."

"Lovely. Very nice. But just a tiny bit light, don't you think?"

"You're going shopping," she said.

I sighed. Used to be I could have strung her on for minutes, clucking how anorexia creeps up on working women, or fretting over the coming ice age and dwindling world food supplies. Now Leslie sees through my craftiest diversion.

Not all had been lost, for I did get to see how much she weighed.

"Want anything special?" Pies and cakes and hot fudge cookies, I hoped she'd say.

"Vegetables and grains," she said, unthinking discipline. "Do we need more carrots?"

"On my list," I said. The day before we decide to ascend out of our bodies, I thought, I'm going to make two lemon pies, one for each of us, and I shall suggest we eat them hot. My wife will decline, shocked at my broken control, and I will have to eat them both.

✦

He found me at the rice section of the grains aisle. "There's a philosophy of flight, isn't there?"

I turned, glad to see him. "Dickie, yes! In order to fly, we have to trust what we can't see, don't we? And the more we learn about the invisible Principle of Aerodynamics the more freedom we gain, till it seems like magic, what we can do when we . . ."

"And there's a philosophy of bowling."

The shift startled me to echo aloud: "Bowling?"

A woman at the cracked-wheat bin glanced up at me standing alone, asking that word, hefting a bag of brown rice. I shook my head and smiled at her for a second: I'm a little eccentric.

Dickie didn't notice. "There has to be," he said. "If there's a philosophy of flight, there's got to be a philosophy of bowling, too, for people who don't like airplanes."

"Captain," I told him silently, wheeling my shopping cart toward the vegetable corner, "there's no such thing as people who don't like airplanes. There is a philosophy of bowling, however: We all choose our turns at the alley, and the fun is to clear it of the pins which are our tests in life, set up time and again. The pins are balanced just so, they have been designed to be knocked down, they were made for the purpose. But they will stand indefinitely at the end of our alley until we decide to take careful action to clear them from our way. A seven-ten split is not a disaster, it's a pleasure, it's a chance to show our discipline and skill and grace under pressure, and those who watch are as delighted as we are when we bring it off."

"Gardening," he said.

"We reap what we sow, of course. Take care which seeds we plant, for the fruit of those seeds will one day become our dinner . . ."

So caught up was I with his test that I wheeled by the chocolate display without a second look, readying my metaphors of sun and weeds and water, planning ahead for his questions about the Philosophy of Pole-Vaulting, of Race-Car Driving, of Retail Sales. In whatever calling we most love, I thought, waits the clearest metaphor and the smoothest path to discover why we chose to play on earth.

"But how does it work, Richard?" At once he gritted his teeth in horror at his mistake. "How do *you think* it works?"

"The universe? I told you." I chose a bag of apples from an open counter.

"Not the universe. The seeds. The way things happen, and why. Not that it matters much, since you say it's all appearances, but how do invisible beliefs get to be visible objects and events?"

"Sometimes I wish you were a grown-up, Dickie."

"Why?"

Interesting, I thought, picking a handful of beets. Not a murmur of distress when I wished for a change impossible for him to make. Had I been emotionally advanced, as well as a bright little guy?

"Because I could explain in a lot fewer words if you knew quantum mechanics. I've whittled the physics of consciousness down to a hundred words, but you're going to have to puzzle over it forever. You're never going to be a grown-up, and I'll never be able to hand you my tract that fits on one page."

Curiosity prevailed. "Pretend I'm a grown-up who loves quantum mechanics," he said. "How would you say how consciousness works in one page? I'm too little to understand, of course, but it would be fun to hear. Say it as complicated as you want."

He's daring me, I thought, he thinks I'm bluffing. I turned the shopping cart toward the checkout stand.

"First I'd say the title:

"The Physics of Consciousness, or, *Spacetime Explained."*

"Next you'd tell me the abstract," he said.

I looked at him. I didn't learn about abstracts until after I had run away from school. How could he know?

228

"Right," I said. "And now I have to talk in fine print, the way they do in *The American Journal of Particle Science*. Listen tight, and maybe you'll understand a word or two, child though you may be."

He laughed. "Child though I may be."

I cleared my throat, slowed the cart and stopped near the cash register, glad for the minute's wait in line. "You want to hear this right straight through, all at once?"

"As if I was a quantum mechanic," he said.

Instead of correcting his grammar, I told him what I thought.

"We are focus–points of consciousness," I said, "enormously creative. When we enter the self-constructed hologrammetric arena we call spacetime, we begin at once to generate creativity particles, *imajons,* in violent continuous pyrotechnic deluge. Imajons have no charge of their own but are strongly polarized through our attitudes and by the force of our choice and desire into clouds of *conceptons,* a family of very-high-energy particles which may be positive, negative or neutral."

He listened, pretended he could understand.

"Some common positive conceptons are *exhilarons, excytons, rhapsodons, jovions.* Common negative conceptons include *gloomons, tormentons, tribulons, agonons, miserons.*

"Indefinite numbers of conceptons are created in nonstop eruption, a thundering cascade of creativity pouring from every center of personal consciousness. They mushroom into *concepton clouds,* which can be neutral or strongly charged—buoyant, weightless or leaden, depending on the nature of their dominant particles.

"Every nanosecond an indefinite number of concepton clouds build to critical mass, then transform in quantum bursts to high-energy probability waves radiating at tachyon speeds through an eternal reservoir of supersaturated alternate events. Depending on their charge and nature, the probability waves crystallize certain of these potential events to match the mental polarity of their creating consciousness into holographic appearance. Are you following, Dickie?"

He nodded, and I laughed.

"The materialized events become that mind's experience, freighted with all the aspects of physical structure necessary to make them real and learningful to the creating consciousness. This autonomic process is the fountain from which springs every object and event in the theater of spacetime.

"The persuasion of the imajon hypothesis lies in its capacity for personal verification. The hypothesis predicts that as we focus our conscious intention on the positive and life-affirming, as we fasten our thought on these values, we polarize masses of positive conceptons, realize beneficial probability-waves, bring useful alternate events to us that otherwise would not have appeared to exist.

"The reverse is true in the production of negative events, as is the mediocre in-between. Through default or intention, unaware or by design, we not only choose but create the visible outer conditions that are most resonant to our inner state of being.

"The end."

He waited while I paid for the groceries. "That's it?" he said.

"Is it wrong?" I asked. "Have I erred in any way?"

He smiled, for Dad had taught us both how important it is to pronounce that word correctly. "How can I tell if you erred, child that I am?"

"Laugh if you must," I told him, "go ahead, call me a zany. But a hundred years from now somebody's going to

231

print those words in *Modern Quantum Theory,* and no-body's going to think it's mad."

He stepped on the frame of the shopping cart, rode along as I pushed it to the car. "If you don't get trapped by gloomons," he said, "that will probably happen."

Thirty-two

I was test-flying Daisy, a long climb to twenty thousand feet, to check the turbochargers at altitude. Lately the engines had been surging, up high, and I hoped as simple a fix as oiling the wastegates would make the difference.

The world moved softly by, two miles down, sinking to four, mountains and rivers and the edge of the sea turned by altitude to an angel's misty painting of home. Daisy's climb speed is faster than the top speed of many a light airplane, but at altitude, looking down, it felt as though she drifted lazy on a lake of deep blue air.

"From everything you've ever learned," Dickie said, "tell me one thing I need to know more than anything, one thing never to forget."

I thought about that. "One thing?"

"Just one."

"What do you know about chess?"

"I like it. Dad taught me when I was seven."

"Do you love your dad?"

He frowned. "No."

"Before he dies, you'll love him for his curiosity and his humor and for living the best he could with a set of stern principles. For now, love him for teaching you chess."

"It's a game."

"So is soccer," I said, "and so is tennis and basketball and ice hockey and so is living."

He sighed. "That's the one thing I need to know? I was expecting something a little more . . . hidden," he said. "I was hoping for your secret. Everybody says that living's a game."

Through sixteen thousand feet, the rear engine revolutions began fluctuating, a gentle rise and fall. No change in fuel flow, but I heard the surge and fade. I eased the propeller control levers ahead and it steadied.

"You want a secret?" I asked. "*Sometimes, on rare occa-*

sions, what everybody says happens to be true. What if everybody's right, and the belief of life on the belief of earth really is a game? Then . . . ?"

He turned to me puzzled. "Then . . . what?"

"Let's say we're here for the sport of learning choices that bring us long-term positive consequence. A tough sport, Dickie, a hard game to win. But if living's a game, tell me what's true about living."

He guessed. "It has rules?"

"Yes," I said. "What rules?"

"You have to show up . . ."

"Absolutely essential. We have to show up, ready to play, consciousness tuned."

He frowned. "Pardon?"

"If we don't tune our consciousness, Captain, we can't play on earth. An all-knowing expression of perfect Life has to reject all-knowingness and claim five senses only. Then we have to agree to limit even those five, perceive certain frequencies and no others. Hear frequencies from twenty cycles to twenty thousand cycles per second and call it *sound;* see the spectrum between infrared and ultraviolet and call it *light;* accept past-to-future linear time in

235

three-dimensional exclusive space in the body of a surface-dwelling carbon-based upright-biped land-mammal life-form adapted to a solar energy-system on a Class M planet orbiting a single Class G star. Now we're ready to play."

"Richard . . ."

"Those are the rules, Dickie, and you and me, we follow them!"

"I don't know about you," he said, "but . . ."

"Have it your way," I said. "Thought experiment: What if you don't limit yourself? What if you can see infrareds and ultraviolets and X rays along with everybody else's visible light? Do houses and parks and people look the same to you as they do to me? Can you and I share a landscape? What if your sight includes angles so small that tabletops are mountain ranges and flies are birds? Is your daily life the same as mine? What if you hear every sound, every conversation in a three-mile radius? How do you pay attention in school? What if you have a body that won't pass for human? What if you remember futures before you were born and pasts that haven't happened? Do you think you're invited to play with the rest of us when you don't follow our rules? Who do you think is going to play with you?"

He tilted his head left, then right. "Okay," he conceded, not nearly so impressed with the rules as I, but warming to his test. "And a game has some kind of play-ground. A board or a field or a court."

"Yes! And?"

"It has players. Or teams."

"Yes. Without us, no game," I said. "What other rules?"

"A beginning. A middle. An ending."

"Yes. And?"

"Action," he said.

"Yes. And?"

"That's it," he said.

"A major rule you forgot," I said. "Roles. Every game we play, we slip into a role, a game identity with which to play. We decide we're rescuer, victim, leader-with-all-the-answers, follower-without-a-clue, bright, brave, honorable, crafty, dull, helpless, just-trying-to-get-along, diabolical, easygoing, pitiable, earnest, careless, salt-of-the-earth, pup-petmaster, comic, hero . . . we choose our role by whim and destiny, and we can change it anytime we want."

"What's your role?" he asked. "Right this minute."

I laughed. "This minute I'm playing the Nice-Enough-Guy-from-Your-Future-with-Some-Pet-Ideas-for-the-Kid-to-Think-About. What's yours?"

"I'm pretending to be the Boy-from-Your-Past-Who-Needs-to-Know-How-the-Universe-Runs." He looked at me in the strangest way as he said this, as if his mask were down, as if he knew I'd see through his role to the truth within. I was too caught up in my own play to look, however, too carried with the fun of the lesson to notice.

"Good," I said. "Now lift yourself out of the play, but keep telling me about the game."

He smiled, knitted his brow. "What do you mean?"

I banked the airplane to the right, pointed to ground, three miles below. "What do you know about games from this height?"

He looked down. "Oh!" he said. "There are a lot of 'em going on at once. Different rooms, different courts, different fields, different cities, different countries . . ."

". . . different planets and galaxies and universes," I said. "Yes! And?"

"Different times!" he said. "Players can play game after game after game." Watching from above, he understood. "We can play on different teams, play for fun or play for keeps, play against somebody easy to beat or go up against somebody there's no chance to win . . ."

"You like to play when you know you can't lose, don't you?"

"NO! The harder it is, the more fun!" He reconsidered. "As long as I win."

"If there were no risk, if you knew you couldn't lose, if you knew the ending, would the game still be fun?"

"The fun's not knowing, at first." He turned to me abruptly. "Bobby knew the ending."

"Was Bobby's life a tragedy, that he died so young?"

He looked out the window, down again. "Yeah. I'll never know who he would have been. Who I would have been."

"Pretend living's a game. Would Bobby think his life was tragedy?"

"Give me a thought experiment."

I smiled at that. "You and Bobby are playing chess in a beautiful house, lots of different rooms. In the middle of the play your brother sees how it's going to end, he can't figure any other way out, he resigns the game and goes off to explore the house. Does he think what happened was a tragedy?"

"It's no fun when you know the end, and he wants to see the other rooms. To him it's no tragedy."

"Is it a tragedy to you, when he leaves?"

"I don't cry," he said, "when somebody leaves the room."

"Now zoom back down to the chessboard. But instead of playing the game, you *are* the game. The chess pieces are named Dickie and Bobby and Mom and Dad and instead of wood they're made out of flesh and blood and you've known each other all your life. Instead of squares there are houses and schools and streets and stores. Now the game turns so that the piece called 'Bobby' is taken. He disappears, completely off the board. Is that a tragedy?"

"Yes! He's not just in another room, he's gone! There's nobody can replace him and I'll have to get along for the rest of my life without him."

"So the closer we get to the game," I said, "and the more caught up in it we are, the more loss feels like tragedy. But loss is tragedy *only for the players,* Dickie, only when we forget it's chess we're playing, when we forget why, when we think our board is the only one that exists."

240

He watched me carefully.

"The more we forget it's play, and we're the players, the more senseless living becomes. But earthlife's the same as baseball and fencing . . . as soon as the game's over, we remember . . . oh, I play because I love the sport!"

"When I forget," he said, "all I have to do is float up over the chessboard and look again?"

I nodded.

"You learned that from airplanes," he said.

"I learned it from altitude. From perching up here and looking down on a lot of chessboards all around the world."

"Somebody dies, you're not sad?"

"Not for them, I'm not," I said. "And not for me, any-more. Grief was a dive into self-pity, and every time I grieved I came out not healed but cold and wet. I couldn't force myself to believe that death in spacetime is any more real than life in spacetime, and after a while I stopped try-ing."

I leveled at twenty thousand feet, pulled the throttles back to cruise power. There was quite a lag from climb power to cruise, but that's normal. The turbocharger wastegates were full closed, blasting white fire direct into the turbines. The sky outside was frozen 20 degrees below zero, the exhaust stacks were torches hot enough to melt silver. On such contrast, I thought, do we fly.

"Most people say mourning's important, Dickie, that grief's healthier than juice of carrot and air of forest. I'm too simple to get it. Grief is no more necessary when we understand death than fear is necessary when we understand flying. Why mourn somebody who hasn't died?"

"It's expected?" he asked. "You're supposed to grieve when people disappear."

"Why?" I said.

"Because you're supposed to stop thinking and give in to what you see and then you're supposed to feel . . . *unhappy* about it! It's the rules, Richard! Everybody does it!"

"Not everybody, Captain. Even grief has to make sense, and until it does why must we grieve? If I could tell you one thing about living, I'd tell you never forget it's a game."

About that time the rear engine began surging again, rpm and manifold pressure and fuel pressure together.

"Rats!" I said, frustrated at the problem.

"It's just a game, Richard."

"Mice," I said, softening my frown. I eased the trim forward and we started back to earth.

"Tell me something else I need to know. Give me some maxims to use every day."

"Maxims," I said. How I've always pleasured when a few words carry so much freight! *"When you pull a propeller through compression, don't be surprised if the engine starts."*

He turned to me, his brow furrowed in questions.

"An aviator's maxim," I said. "The Rule of Unintended Consequences. In twenty years you'll know how profound it is.

"Every real teacher is myself in disguise."

"Is that true?" he said.

"Dickie, would you like to own some first-class maxims?"

"Yes, please."

"I'm sorting my life this minute to give you free the best I know, earned at the price of all my days. You're infinitely intelligent. If you don't understand them now, I expect you to figure them out later, on your own time."

"Yes, sir," meek like a Zen student.

"Shop for security over happiness and we buy it at that price.

"There's no sound when a tree falls unheard in the forest, and there's no spacetime without consciousness nearby to watch.

"Guilt is the tension we feel to change our past, present or future for someone else's sake.

"Some choices we live not once but a thousand times over, remembering for the rest of our lives."

Lucky for us we aren't aware of other lifetimes, I thought. Immobilized by memories, we couldn't get on with this one.

"We know nothing till intuition agrees."

The rear engine stabilized as we sank through sixteen thousand feet. Something in that turbocharger is not a lot wrong, I thought, it's just a little bit wrong.

"Get this in mind early: We never grow up.

"All we see of someone at any moment is a snapshot of their

life, there in riches or poverty, in joy or despair. Snapshots don't show the million decisions that led to that moment."

"Thank you, Richard," said Dickie. "Those are fine maxims. I think I've got enough."

"The mildest suggestion for change is a death-threat to some status quo.

"Compelling reason will never convince blinding emotion.

"Life does not require us to be consistent, cruel, patient, helpful, angry, rational, thoughtless, loving, rash, open-minded, neurotic, careful, rigid, tolerant, wasteful, rich, downtrodden, gentle, sick, considerate, funny, stupid, healthy, greedy, beautiful, lazy, responsive, foolish, sharing, pressured, intimate, hedonistic, industrious, manipulative, insightful, capricious, wise, selfish, kind or sacrificed. Life does, however, require us to live with the consequences of our choices."

"Well," he said. "I'll bet that takes a toll, sorting through your lifetime. Thank you. That's a lot of maxims!"

"Alternate lives are landscapes reflected in window-glass . . . they're as real as our daily lives, but not so clearly seen.

"If it's never our fault, we can't take responsibility for it. If we can't take responsibility for it, we'll always be its victim."

"Thank you, Richard."

"Our true country is the land of our values," I continued, *"and our conscience is the voice of its patriotism.*

"We don't have rights until we claim them.

"We must honor our dragons, encourage them to be worthy destroyers, expect they'll strive to cut us down. It is their duty to ridicule us, it is their job to demean us, to force us if they can to stop being different! *And when we walk our way no matter their fire and their fury, our dragons shrug when we're out of sight, return to their card-games philosophical: 'Ah well, we can't toast 'em all . . . '*

"When we put up with any situation that we don't have to put up with, it's not because we're dumb. We put up with it because we want the lesson that only that situation can teach, and we want it more than freedom itself.

"Happiness is the reward we get for living to the highest right we know."

"THAT'S ENOUGH! THAT'S TOO MANY, RICH-ARD! STOP THE MAXIMS IF YOU SAY ONE MORE MAXIM I'M GOING TO POP!"

"Okay," I said. "But be careful what you pray for, Dickie, becau—"

"AAAAAAAAAAAAAIIIIIIIIIIEEEEEEEEEEEEEEEE!!!!"

Thirty-three

*W*hile I scrambled our dinner, Leslie perched on a long-legged counter-chair, listening bemused to my adventures with Dickie.

"From here he's just my little imaginary pal," I said, "and I tell him everything I know for the fun of remembering it myself." I tilted a board of chopped everything from the vegetable bin into our big frying pan.

"Are you hiding behind 'imaginary'?" said Leslie. "Do you need a safe distance? Are you afraid of him?" She had stopped on her way to change from gardening clothes: white shorts, T-shirt, wide-brim sun-hat. She had taken off her hat, but now she was snared by curiosity, looking deeper for meanings, and I suspected the change would have to wait.

"Afraid?" I said. "Maybe so." I doubted that, but from

time to time it's fun to test our certainties, pretend they're lies. "What could he say to hurt me?"

I added the pineapple to the pan on the stove, bulgur wheat, five or six quick stirs.

"He could say he invented you, decide you're only an imaginary future, walk away and leave you with everything you need to tell him unsaid."

I looked up at her, no smile, forgot to tilt the soy sauce bottle, so of course it didn't pour. "He wouldn't do that. Not now."

Once it wouldn't have mattered if he left me, I thought. Now it would.

She let her question simmer, and went on. "Does he notice you're cooking and I'm not?" she said. "Does he care?"

"I cook for my wife, I tell him, but I'm very masculine . . . even my pastries are tough!" Not true, of course. Before I gave up sugar, I made pies. Delicate as baked cloud, those crusts, but I'm more modest than God. That noble quality in which I take greatest pride is my complete lack of ego.

It's important that the wheat gets plenty hot, they say;

the heat brings out a nutty flavor. Just in case, I found a half-bag of chopped walnuts, added them to the pan.

Leslie knows my odd principles as well as anyone who doesn't think they're true, but she's tolerant and sometimes likes to hear more. "What have you told him about marriage?" she said.

"He hasn't asked. Think he'd be interested?"

"He knows that marriage is waiting, up ahead. If he's you, he'll ask," she said. "What are you going to say?"

"I'll say it's the happiest hardest most important long-term challenge of his life." I lifted a teaspoon of toasted dinner from the pan for her to taste. It's not cooked yet, I thought, but it never hurts to be courteous to one's soulmate. "Wouldn't you?"

"Too crunchy," she said. "It's awfully dry."

"Mm." I lifted the pan from the stove to the kitchen sink, opened the faucet for a cup or so, set it back on the fire to perk for ten heaping minutes.

"Can I help?" she asked.

"Sweet thing. You've been working. Stay put."

She went to the cupboard, brought out plates and forks. "What are you going to tell him?"

"I'd tell him my secret of marriage first, then fill him in on the facts." I found the juicer and plugged it in, fetched a raft of carrots from the refrigerator.

She smiled at me. "You *are* wise! What's your secret of marriage?"

"Now, come on, Wookie, don't kid me on wise. I told him I'd say what I knew." I set a glass under the juicer spout.

"Okay," she said. "You're not wise. What's your secret of marriage?"

I touched the switch and pressed in the first carrot. The juice is from paradise, but our machine is a noisy devil on the job.

"IT'S OKAY FOR YOU TO DO WHAT YOU THINK IS RIGHT," I said over the gnash of spinning cutters. "IT'S OKAY FOR YOUR WIFE TO DO WHAT SHE THINKS IS RIGHT. AND IT'S OKAY WHEN YOU DON'T AGREE!"

"I DISAGREE!" she said. "ACCORDING TO THAT, IT WOULD BE OKAY FOR US TO CHEAT ON EACH OTHER, LIE TO EACH OTHER, ABUSE

EACH OTHER IN ANY WAY WE THOUGHT WAS 'RIGHT'! YOU HAVE TO ADD THAT THE REASON YOUR SECRET WORKS IS BECAUSE WE HAVE YEARS OF TRUSTING EACH OTHER, YEARS OF KNOWING THE CHARACTER OF THE PARTNER WITH WHOM WE ARE DEALING! I KNOW IT'S OKAY FOR YOU TO DO WHAT YOU THINK IS RIGHT BECAUSE YOUR SENSE OF RIGHT AND MINE ARE VERY MUCH THE SAME!"

The juicer is as fast as it is loud. The second glass was full and I pressed the switch to *off*.

"Don't you agree?" she said in the sudden quiet.

"No." I sipped my carrots. "It is always okay for us to do what we believe is right. No exceptions."

She laughed at my contrariness, and I was forced to smile a little, myself.

"Would your secret have saved your first marriage?"

I shook my head. "It was too late. When you become dehumanized by a marriage, it's time to end it. She and I disagreed so much that it was not okay to be who we wanted to be anymore. We didn't merely stop loving each other, we couldn't stand to be in the same room. There's no cure for that."

"I remember times when you and I couldn't stand to be in the same room," she teased. She had the lid off the frying pan, trying dinner again with her spoon. "You think we should have ended it?"

"You're hungry, aren't you?" I said.

She nodded, eyes wide. "Hot . . ."

"It'll only be a minute," I told her, turning the fire off early. "You were different, Wookie. Those days, even when I was furious at you, I couldn't forget you're so damned terrific. Times I'd walk out of the house, wrecked that you didn't understand who I was or what I was thinking or how I was feeling. I'd shout in the car, driving away: *Dear God how can you expect me to live with Leslie Parrish? It's impossible! It can't be done!* And even in that moment I knew you were smart as hell, you were still so beautiful that it hurt. Divorce was inevitable, and I loved you anyway. Isn't that strange?"

I took the pan to the table, served our vejiwheat for two.

"Oh, Richie, divorce was never inevitable," she said. "It was only a desperation thought."

Defending outdated conclusions, I thought, is not a sign of wisdom, and even if it is I won't. Divorce was inevitable doesn't matter.

If we must lose wife or husband when we live to our highest right, we lose an unhappy marriage as well, and we gain ourselves. But if a marriage is born between two already self-discovered, what a lovely adventure begins, hurricanes and all!

"As soon as I stopped expecting you always to understand," I said, "when I learned that it is all right for you and me to have different ideas and different conclusions, and that it's all right for each of us to do whatever we need to do about that, a road opened through the dead end. I wasn't trapped by your conclusions, you weren't trapped by my differences."

"True," she said. "And thank you for dinner. It's delicious."

"Did I add too much heat? You said it was hot."

"It's better now." She sipped her liquid carrot. "And Dickie may not ask about marriage."

"He'll ask," I said. "He'll say why do you think we're here? And I'll tell him I think we're here to express love, a million different tests for us to show it, a million more when we fail, a million more when we pass. And nowhere more tests, every minute of every day, than in year after year of intimate daily life with one other soul."

"That's sweet," she said. "I didn't know you thought marriage was so important."

"Not marriage," I said. "Love is that important."

"I'm glad to hear you say that. I think you're wonderful, but you're also the least loving man I know, sometimes. I have never met anyone, man or woman, who can be as cold or uncaring as you can be. Thorns in ice, when you feel threatened."

I shrugged. "So I've got a little way to go. I'm not saying I pass my tests, only that I know they're there. Patience. I'll find my way to a lifetime where I'm the kind of dear soul that a lot of people already are. For now I'm happier being who I am. Suspicious, armored, defensive . . ."

"Oh, you're not that bad," she said brightly. "You haven't been suspicious for a long time."

"I'm fishing for compliments!" I said. "Not even a nibble?"

"Tell Dickie that I think you're not the worst man in the world."

"When you're mad at me, you think I am."

"No. Not even close," she said. "What else are you going to tell him about marriage?"

"The difference between marriage and ceremony," I said. "I'll tell him real marriage isn't two people dashing across a bridge in rice and ribbons, it's discovering after a lifetime that they've built the bridge together, with their own hands."

She put down her fork. "Richie, that's beautiful!"

"I should talk to you instead of Dickie," I said.

"Talk to us both," she said. "When it makes you happier, I get to live with a happy man."

"I'd tell him that, too. Wives and husbands do not have the power to make each other happy or unhappy. That's an individual power. Each can make only herself or himself happy."

"On one level that's true, but if you're saying nothing we do impacts the other, I disagree with you completely."

"The impacts," I said, "are our tests for each other. You can decide to be happy yourself no matter what I do, and chances are that when you're happy I'll be glad, because I like being with you when you're happy. But it's *me* making me happy, not you."

She shook her head and smiled forbearance at me. "Such a strange way of looking at things."

She thought it was a detail, some fine point of logic for me, blocking a gift of her love. I felt like a rhino heading for thin ice, but I had to make it clear.

"If you're not feeling well," I said, "but you decide you're going to make me happy by fixing dinner for me or going out with me, do you expect it to work, do you expect me to be happy when I know you're feeling terrible?"

"I wouldn't let you know I felt terrible, and yes, I'd expect you to be happy."

"But then you'd be a martyr. You'd 'make me happy' only by sacrificing yourself, by lying to me, by faking happiness for my sake. If it worked, I'd be happy not because you were happy, but because I believed you were. It's not you or what you do for me, it's *my belief* that makes me happy. And my beliefs are my responsibility, not yours."

"That sounds so cold," she said. "If that's the case, why should I make any effort to please you?"

"When you don't want to, you shouldn't try! Remember when you were working eighteen hours a day in the office with the flood of work we had?"

"Our work, but I was doing it all?" she said sweetly. "Yes, I remember."

"And do you remember how thankful I was, how grateful?"

"Of course I do. You sat there with a big scowl on your face, grudging and resentful, as if you were the one being worked to death!"

"Remember how long that went on?"

"Years."

"And because you were doing my work for me, things got so loving between us?"

"I seem to recall that toward the end of that period I couldn't stand you! I'm working dawn to midnight, you blithely announce that you're going off to fly for a while, you've had too much office work. You're lucky I didn't kill you!"

The more time we spend at work we hate, I thought, the less joy we'll have in our marriage.

"But finally something snapped," I said. "You said screw this work, screw goddamned selfish Richard Bach, I'm going to get my life back. I don't care about him, I'm going to care about me, I'm going to have *fun*."

"I did, too!" she said, eyes turning merry mischief.

"What happened?"

She laughed. "The happier I got, the better you liked it!"

"There! Hear what you said? You chose to be happy yourself!"

"I did."

"But I got happier when you did," I said, "even when you weren't trying to Make Me Happy."

"Sure enough."

I tapped the table, my finger for a gavel. "I rest my case."

"I suppose you were trying to make me happy," she said, "by telling me not to work so long and so hard in the office."

"Of course I was. Back in the days when I tried to solve your problems for you."

"Telling me to stop then was stupid," she said. "I can stop work and have fun today because we're at a different point in our lives. The work we do today is chosen work, not life-and-death stuff. We can do it or ignore it, as we wish. Those days our work was serious business—getting you out of the tangle of legal and financial problems you had when I met you, if you'll recall. And without all my work, you wouldn't be in such a comfortable position today. At best, you would have had to leave this country, and I don't want to consider what might have happened to you at worst. So, with the stakes that high, I chose to work like crazy. If you'd wanted to make me happy then, you could have pitched in and helped!"

"But don't you see? I didn't want to! Getting work done wasn't important to me! I didn't care if it never was done! Those few times I tried to help you, I was unhappy, resentful, and that just made it worse."

"So of course I chose to do even more of it myself," she said, "rather than have some thorny hostile troll trying to 'help,' making a mess of it because he's so resentful."

"Not of course. You had other choices. But even though I was trying to Make You Happy, it didn't work because I wasn't happy myself."

"You're right, I did have other choices. I should have let your problems catch up with you and flatten you. Then you would have learned the lesson from them instead of me learning a lesson I already knew. From that, I learned this: If you mess up again, I won't deprive you of any future lessons. But, in fact, you weren't trying to make me happy, you were trying to make you happy, just as you are now."

Uh-oh, I thought. Was dinner-talk brewing into a storm?

"The difference between now and then," she said, "is that our lives have changed, and in today's calm and comfort, both of us have a chance at happiness. You seem to think it's because I suddenly chose to work less and play more. You choose to believe I worked for work's sake, I guess, and that I've come to my senses at last. I think you lived in fantasy-land all those years because you couldn't cope with the enormous problems you'd created. Whatever the truth, I'm enjoying life too much to argue the point further."

I crafted my response for a moment in silence. We lived those years together, but our convictions were so different that today we remember different pasts.

"Is this for Dickie," she asked, sea-blue eyes into mine, "or is it for us? Are you going to tell him about our fights?"

"Maybe not. Maybe I should tell him that a perfect marriage has no fights. Perfection is when two people look at each other and say, 'We knew it all before the marriage. No fights, no tests, neither one of us changed in fifty years. Didn't learn a thing.' "

The picture made her smile. "Deadly dull stuff," she said. "Avoid problems and you'll never be the one who overcame them."

"He needs to know. Telling marriage-lessons is a re-minding for me; Dickie has to make what he can from it, keep some and throw the rest away. I'll tell him the best I've figured out: Don't ever assume that your wife is a mind-reader, that she understands who you are, or that she knows what you think or how you feel. To make that as-sumption is to ask for terrible pain. She might understand, she might know from time to time, but don't expect her to understand you one bit more than you understand her. Decide to be happy by doing what you want to do. If your happiness makes her angry, or if you hate it when she's joyful, then you don't have a marriage, you have an experi-ment that was doomed from the start."

"That makes it sound like marriage is as much fun as jumping off a cliff. Is that what you want him to think?"

"Marriage is like nothing else you'll ever live, I'll tell him, brought together by miraculous magnetizing, found by incredible coincidence, soulmates discovered in the mystery of romance, you still have to work out problems together. Fascinating problems, it's true, spicy tests lasting year after year, but lose romance and you lose the power to go on through hard times, learning to love. Lose romance and you'll never learn, you'll fail at love. Fail at love, the other tests don't matter."

"What about children?"

"I'm not qualified to tell him anything," I said. "Next?"

"What do you mean you're not qualified, next? You have children, and surely you've learned something from them! What are you going to tell him?"

My weak point, I thought. I'm as useful around children as an anvil in a nursery.

"I'll tell him that inner guidance doesn't come to adults only," I said. "We experience what we bring to ourselves no matter what age. That the only guidance we give to children is our own example of the highest most advanced human being we know how to be. Children may understand, they may not. They may love us for our choices, they may curse the ground on which we tread. But children are not our property, and they are not ours to control any more than we were our parents' property or theirs to control."

"Do you feel like an iceberg when you say that," Leslie said, "or does it just sound like forty below zero to me?"

"It's not true?"

"It may have some basis in truth," she soothed. "Certainly we don't own our children, but I sense something's missing. Could it be a little tenderness?"

"Well, of *course* I'll tell him tenderly!"

She shook her head, hopeless, and moved on. "There's more than one secret to marriage."

"What?" I have one secret, I thought, could she have another?

"When you look at us," she said, "when you look at anybody long-term, we really love only once or twice in our lives. Treasure that love. That's my secret of marriage."

Thirty-four

When dinner was finished and the dishes put away, I threw my paraglider into the car and drove toward the mountain. On the way, I reached out in my mind, looking for my little friend.

He sat on the same hilltop, but now there were trees on the slopes, young ones, and a meadow that overlooked a green horizon.

He turned to me the instant I saw him. "Tell me about marriage."

"Of course. Why?"

"I never believed it will happen to me but now I know it will. I'm unprepared."

I suppressed my smile. "Unprepared is all right."

He frowned, impatient. "What do I need to know?"

"One word," I said. "Remember one word and you'll be fine. Remember *different*. You are different from everyone else in the world and you are different from the woman that you will marry."

"I bet you're telling me something simple because you thought it was simple, too, and it turned out it wasn't."

"Simple isn't obvious, Captain. *We're different* is a revelation that a lot of marriages never reach, a realization that doesn't show up for a lot of smart people till years after the dust of divorce has settled."

"Different but equal?"

"Not at all," I said. "Marriage is not an arena of equality. Leslie is better than I am in music, for instance. I will never catch up with what she knew when she was twelve, let alone what she's learned by now. I could study for the rest of my life and never know music as well as she does, or make mine as lovely as hers. On the other hand, she'll probably never fly airplanes better than I do. She started twenty years after I did and she can't catch up."

"Everything else is unequal, too?"

"Everything. I'm not as organized as she is, she's not as patient as I am. She's the fighter for issues that matter to her, I'm the detached observer. I'm selfish, which to me means *acting in my own long-term best interests;* she hates selfish, which to her means *instant gratifying in spite of consequences.* She expects me sometimes to sacrifice my sense of right for hers and she's surprised when I don't.''

"So you're different," he said. "Isn't every husband and wife?"

"And nearly every wife and husband forgets. When I forget and expect Leslie to be selfish, when she forgets and expects me to be organized, we assume the other's as good as we are at skills we've already mastered. That's not going to happen. Marriage isn't a competition to top each other's strengths, it's a cooperation that needs our differences.''

"But sometimes being different drives you crazy, I bet," he said.

"No. Sometimes forgetting that we're different drives us crazy. When I assumed that Leslie was me in another body, that she knew what I was thinking every second and that my values and priorities were hers exactly, I was asking for a barrel-ride over some monster waterfalls. I kept assuming, and I kept wondering the next minute why I'm suddenly down the river and what are these smashed hoops and staves dangling around my neck while I pick myself like a ragged sponge, dripping, off the rocks? I felt guilty, of all things, till I faced it, remembered we're different, and let it go.''

He narrowed his eyes. "Guilty? Why guilty?"

"Remember your maxims," I said. "Guilt is the tension to change our past or present or future for someone else's sake. Guilt is to marriage as the iceberg was to the *Titanic*. Hit it in the dark and you're sunk."

His voice turned wistful. "I was sort of hoping the woman I marry would be a little bit like me."

"No! Hope she's not, Dickie! In two ways Leslie and I are the same: we both agree that our spouse has a few misplaced values and thoughtless priorities. We also agree that we're more in love with each other than we were when we met. Everything else, we're more or less different."

He was unconvinced. "I'm not sure that going over the falls would make me love anybody more."

"It wasn't Leslie who nailed me in the barrel, Cap, it was me! I thought I knew her, I look back now . . . how could I have been so witless? She made some assumptions about me equally off-target, sure enough, but what fun to have come such a long way with the person you love! Year after year with her, even storms are fun, when they're past. I put my arm around her in the night, sometimes, and I'm sure we've just met, we're just beginning to say hello!"

"Hard to figure," he said.

"Can't be figured, Dickie, I don't think. Has to be lived. I wish you patience and skill."

I left him in the quiet, to consider that. It was only later that I realized I had forgotten to tell him my secret of marriage.

Thirty-five

*E*very structure is consciousness. Aircraft are living creatures when we believe they are. When I wash Daisy, polish her, and see to the care of every squeak before it becomes a scream, then the day may come when she might return the favor, when she'll lift into the air before flight is possible, if she has to, or land in an impossibly short space. In forty years' flying this has happened once, and I'm not so sure I'll never need the kindness again.

So it was not strange for me to be lying on the concrete floor of our hangar that morning, wiping three hours of engine exhaust and oil-film from Daisy's aluminum belly.

Every night we change consciousness when we drift into sleep, I thought, dipping my rag lightly in gasoline, but every day we change it as well, whenever we do one thing and think about another. Sleep and wake, dream and daydream a hundred times a day, who counts these as altered states?

All I saw was jeans from the knees down, but the feet were laced into old-fashioned tennis shoes, and I knew who it was.

"Is everything your personal responsibility?" Dickie asked. "Everything in your life? You carry the whole weight?"

"Everything," I said, glad he had found me. "There's no such thing as the masses, there are only us plain old individuals, making our plain old lives however we plain old want. It's not heavy, Dickie. The responsibility for everything is fun to carry, and we individuals do a brisk business, helping each other out."

He sat down on the floor, crossed his legs, watched me work. "Such as?"

"Such as the grocer who makes it easy to find food for the table. Such as the moviemaker who tells us stories, the carpenter who nails a roof over our heads, the airplane builder who puts beautiful Daisy on the market."

"And if Daisy didn't exist, you'd build her yourself?"

"If I had to build my own airplane, it would be smaller than Daisy, probably. A hang glider, an ultralight."

I touched my rag to the can of polishing compound. Just a little will rub away the worst exhaust-stains.

"You're responsible for finding food, even if there were no stores?"

"Who else will do it for me?"

"You'd kill cows yourself?"

As I polished I noticed that there was a split in the fiber-glass, started at a strut-cuff near the distance-measuring antenna. Nothing dangerous, but I made a note to drill the crack and bond it.

"Leslie and I don't eat cows anymore, Dickie. We wouldn't kill one ourselves, and we're deciding that if we don't give our consent to the steps in any process, we'd just as soon not give it to the result."

He thought about that. "You don't wear leather?"

"I'll never own another leather coat, probably not another leather belt, but I might buy leather shoes again if there's no other choice. Then again I might get up to the counter with my shoe-box and not be able to go through with buying. It's a slow process, changing principles, and we don't know they've changed until something that used to be right just doesn't feel that way anymore."

He nodded, expecting that. "Everything's individual."

"Yes."

"You're responsible for your own education?" he said.

"I look to me to provide the education I want, yes."

"Your entertainment?"

"Keep going," I said.

"Your air, your water, your job . . ."

". . . my travel, my attitude, my communication, my health, my protection, my goals, my philosophy and religion, my success and failure, my marriage, my happiness, my life and death. I'm answerable to me for what I think, for every word I say and every move I make. Like it or not it's true, so a long time ago I decided to like it." Where was he going with his questions, I wondered. Was he testing me?

I rubbed the polished paint with wax, carefully around the vortex generators jutting like a fence of knives, more briskly near the radio antennas, sweeping long strokes over the rest. Curiosity or test, I decided, I want him to know.

"So everything in the world of appearances you do for

yourself," he said. "You, personally, built your entire civilization?"

"I did, thank you," I said. "Don't you want to know how?"

He laughed. "You'd fall over if I didn't."

"It wouldn't matter," I lied. "Okay, I'd fall over."

"Tell me. How did you personally build your entire civilization?"

"You and I chose to be born in this belief of place and time, Dickie, and then we stood at the gate of consciousness, screening, deciding whether to engage or withdraw from every suggestion, from every idea and advancement and destruction that our time offers. Reading yes, running-away-from-home no, animal dolls yes, trusting parents yes, believing war propaganda yes, airplane models yes, team sports no, punctuality yes, ice cream yes, carrots no, homework yes, smoking no, drinking no, selfishness yes, drugs no, cutting class no, courtesy yes, smug self-confidence yes, hunting no, guns yes, gangs no, girls yes, school spirit no, college no, military yes, politics no, service-to-others no, marriage yes, children yes, military no, divorce yes, remarriage no, remarriage yes, carrots yes . . . We paint a perfect unique digital portrait of who we shall be, each *yes* every *no* is one tiny dot of our picture. The more decisive we are, the clearer our painting.

273

"Everything in the world of my consciousness, which is the only world that exists for me on earth, gets there through my consent. Whatever I don't care for, I'm free to change. So there's no whining, no complaining that I'm suffering because somebody else let me down. I'm the one to fix it, not them."

"What do you do when somebody else lets you down?"

"I kill them," I said, "and I move on."

He laughed, nervously. "You're kidding, aren't you?"

"We can no more destroy life than we can create it," I said. "Life Is, remember."

I finished the belly, crawled out from under the airplane and fetched a ladder for the vertical stabilizers, nine feet off the ground.

"In the world of appearances," he asked gingerly, "have you ever killed anybody?"

"Yes. I've killed flies, I've killed mosquitoes, I've killed ants and sad to say I've killed spiders, too. I killed fish, when I was not much older than you. Indestructible expressions of life, every one, but I believed I was killing them and that belief drags me down, it sorrows me still, until I remember what's true."

He chose his words carefully. "Have you killed any human beings, in the world of appearances?"

"No, Dickie, I haven't." Thanks to brilliant timing, I thought. A few years earlier to the Air Force, I would have been killing people in Korea. A few years later, I would have been killing them in Vietnam, in the time before I said no to other people's commands.

"Have you ever been killed?"

"Never. Before time was born, I am, after time has stopped, I shall be."

He chafed, exasperated. "In the world of appearances, has your belief of yourself as a limited . . ."

"Oh, *that* world!" I said. "I've been killed a thousand million trillion times, an indefinite number of times!"

Dickie climbed the ladder to the horizontal stabilizer, walked on it a few feet from the rudder and sat to face me, ankles crossed, leaning into his curiosity. No other child could have perched there without my clucking fears about tennis shoes against the paint, stress on the stabilizer, five-foot falls to a concrete floor. But Dickie was welcome to sit where he would. Such are the pleasures of discarnates, I thought, it's a wonder we don't invite them more often.

"That's reincarnation," he said. "Do you believe in re-incarnation?"

I sprayed the top half of the rudder with liquid wax, rubbed it clean.

"No. Reincarnation is a series of lifetimes, isn't it, one after the other, in order, on this planet? That feels a little limiting, it fits a little tight across the shoulders."

"What fits you better?"

"An infinite number of beliefs of life experiences, please, some in bodies, some not; some on planets, some not; all of them simultaneous because there is no such thing as time, none of them real because there's only one Life."

He frowned. "Why is infinite-life-experiences true and not reincarnation?"

Long ago, I remembered, that was my favorite question: Why this way and not that way? Drove a lot of grown-ups crazy, as I recall, but I had to know.

"Infinite-life-experiences is no more true than reincarnation," I told him. "Until we recognize Life Is, we don't merely believe in reincarnation, or infinite life experiences, or heaven-and-hell, or everything-goes-black, we *live* those systems . . . they're true for us, every minute we give them power.''

"Then I don't understand. Why don't you recognize Life Is, and stop playing games?"

"I *like* games! If anyone doubts this life is for the fun of it, offer her or him a detailed account of their personal future . . . every event, every ending, years before it comes. How long before they beg you to stop? It is not fun to know what happens next. I like chess, even when I know it's a game. I like spacetime even though it isn't real."

"Help!" he said. "If none of it's real, why choose infinite life experiences instead of everybody-turns-into-angels or reincarnation?"

"Why chess instead of checkers?" I said. "There are more combinations to play! If all my beliefs-of-lifetimes are simultaneous, for instance, then there's got to be some way for them to meet in person. There's got to be some way to find the Richard who chose China in the now I call seven thousand years ago, the one who became a boat builder in 1954 instead of a flyer, the one who chose to be a Proximid and picked a life in the space fleets of Centauri Four in the now a billion years from today. If all time is Now, there ought to be a way for us to talk. What do they know that I don't?"

A curious look on his face, a hidden smile. "Any luck so far?"

"Flickers here and there," I said.

"Hm." He smiled again that strange smile, as though he were the teacher here, and not me. I should have asked him then, what's so funny? But I let it pass, thinking he wasn't convinced, remembering not to care. Let him make his own mind.

"But proof is not required," I said, climbing down to reset the ladder near the left stabilizer leading edge. "Life doesn't limit our freedom to believe in limits. Until we let go our romance with form, I'll bet we wake from one limiting belief into another into another, outgrowing spacetime the way we outgrow our play with blocks, no matter what color, no matter what shape they came in, to find our pleasures in other toys."

"Toys? For the indefinite future?" he said. "I thought I was ahead of you. I thought you were going to tell me the next life is unconditional love."

"Nope. Unconditional love is no more a force in space-time than it is in chess, or soccer, or ice hockey. Rules define life in games, and unconditional love doesn't recognize rules."

"Name a rule," he said.

"Let's see . . ." I finished the left, climbed down and moved the ladder to the right stabilizer, climbed up and sprayed wax on the leading edge. "Self-preservation's a rule. The minute we no longer care whether we live or die, the minute we shift our values outside spacetime, all at once we can love unconditionally."

"Really?"

"Try it," I said. I waxed the leading edge, buffed it out.

"How?"

The vertical stabilizers sparkled, twin ivory sculpture in the hangar. I moved to the horizontal stabilizer.

"Pretend you're an advanced soul, a peaceful nonviolent leader, and you've vowed to free your enslaved nation from a tyrant. You promise the tyrant you will call for giant protest-rallies in the capital until he resigns."

"I tell him that? I may be advanced," said Dickie, "but I'm none too smart, am I?"

I smiled. My father used to say that: *none too smart.*

"You're warned," I said. "The tyrant's men are on the way, they're coming to kill you. Are you frightened?"

"Yes!" said Dickie. "Where do I run?"

"Nowhere. You're an advanced soul, remember. So right now, this minute, let go of self-preservation, let go of rules, stop caring whether you live or die. This is a world of appearances and you have a different home, a deeper known-and-loved than earth, to which you will be glad to return."

I polished around Dickie as he sat high on the stabilizer, eyes closed, pretending. "Okay," he said, "I've stopped caring. I don't want anything, I don't need anything from earth. I'm ready to go home."

"Here come the assassins to your door. Are you frightened?"

"No," he said, dreaming. "They're not my killers, they're my friends. We're actors in a play. We choose our parts, we play them out."

"They're drawing their swords. Do you fear them?"

"I love them," he said.

"There," I said. "Now you know what unconditional love feels like. You don't have to be a saint, anyone can do it; let go of spacetime and it doesn't matter whether they kill you or not."

In a minute Dickie opened his eyes, moved to the end of

the stabilizer so I could polish the place where he had been.

"Interesting. Does it work the other way? The more I care about self-preservation, the less I feel unconditional love?"

"Want to find out?"

"Okay." He closed his eyes, waiting.

"Pretend you're a farmer, peaceful, gentle," I said. "You have three loves: your family and your land and your fields of daffodils. You and your wife are raising your children and your flowers in the same valley that was cleared and plowed by your parents before you. You were born on this land and here you plan to die."

"Uh-oh," he said. "Something's going to happen."

"Yep. Cattle-drivers, Dickie. They want your farm for a shortcut to the railhead, and you didn't sell it to them when they asked. They threatened trouble and you didn't run away. Now they've given you fair warning: at noon today they're taking your farm by force. Get off your land, leave your flowers to die or you'll die, too."

"Oh, my," he said, eyes closed, dreaming again.

"Are you frightened?"

"Yes."

"It's nearly noon, Dickie. They're coming now, on horseback, a dozen armed men in a cloud of dust, firing their revolvers, stampeding a herd of longhorns toward your green fields. Do you love these men unconditionally?"

"NO!" he said.

"So you see . . ."

"I've got my neighbors posted out," he said. "Every one of us with repeating rifles; I've got dynamite buried down the fence-lines. Step on my flowers, tough-guys, you're gonna have one mighty fast Reverse Stampede! You dare trample us, it'll be the last trampling you ever try!"

"You get the idea," I said, smiling at his lightning defense. "See how different from unconditional . . ."

"Don't stop now," he said. "Let me blow 'em up!"

I laughed. "Dickie, this is a thought experiment, not a massacre!"

He opened his eyes. *"Boom . . ."* he said sullenly. "Nobody takes my land!"

I grinned at his frown, lifted him to the top of the fuselage and moved the ladder to begin polishing Daisy's right wing.

"So the only way for Love to be unconditional," he said at last, "is when it doesn't care about our games."

"Doesn't care about games, doesn't care about change-based goals," I said. "Not self-preservation, not justice, not rescue, not morals, not improvement, not education, not progress. It loves who we are, not who we pretend to be. That's why dying is such a shock, I think. The contrast between the role and the real is sharpest, right then. Near-death survivors come back, they say it's love like a sledge-hammer."

"Love for cattle-drivers as much as flower-farmers?"

"The killed and the killers, the meek and the monsters. The same. Absolute. Total. Unconditional. Love."

Dickie lay down on the fuselage, his face turned side-ways on the cool metal, watching me work. "All these things you're telling me? How did you learn 'em?"

"I was hoping you might know," I said. "As long as I can remember, it's mattered to me: *How does the universe run?* When did that start?"

I expected him to hand me an old memory, but if he knew where curiosity came from, he wasn't telling.

"How do you know you're right, with your answers?" he said.

"I don't. But every question's a tension inside, a little electric shock, and it crackles through me till it finds an answer. When a question touches an answer, it grounds on intuition, there's a blue flash, the tension's gone. It doesn't say right or wrong, it just says answered."

Grf, I thought in the quiet, there's a dent in the leading edge . . . we must have hit a pocket of heavy air, last flight.

"Give me an example," he said.

I buffed lightly on the wing, remembering.

"When I was barnstorming," I said, "hopping rides out of Midwest pastures in my old Fleet biplane, for a while I felt guilty. Was it fair for me to be living this life, flying free on the wind and making a living at it, when other people have to work nine-to-five for a living? Everybody can't be a barnstormer, I thought."

"That was your question?" he said.

"That was my tension, same as a question, humming through my mind for weeks: everybody can't be a barn-stormer. Why aren't I stressed-out like everybody else? Is it fair, for me to be so privileged?"

He didn't see the picture as funny, some ratty oil-covered transient sleeping under an airplane wing, chugging rides for dollar bills and fretting why he was the luckiest guy in the world.

"What was your answer?" he asked, solemn as a barn owl.

"I'd think about it at night, all alone, baking my pan-bread over the fire. Barnstorming's a grand romantic profession, I thought, but so's the law, or acting. If everyone were actors, we'd open the Yellow Pages and there'd be just one listing, one category: *A* for Actor. No flight instructors, no toy makers, no attorneys, no police or doctors or retail stores or construction companies, no studios, no producers. Just actors. And finally I understood. Everybody can't be a barnstormer. Everybody can't be a lawyer or an actor or a house painter, either. Everybody can't do *any* one thing!"

"That was your answer?"

"Like a whale leaped from way deep underwater came this great burst and splash in my mind, Dickie: Everybody can't do any one thing, *but anybody can!*"

"Oh," he said, the splash hitting him as well.

"From then on I stopped thinking it wasn't fair that I get to be the person I choose to be." I buffed the wing in

285

silence, yet still he listened on, turning the idea over in his mind.

"Can I be anyone I want?" he asked. "Even if it isn't you?"

"Especially if it isn't me," I told him. "I screw it up from time to time, but my job's taken. Everybody's job is taken, Captain, except yours."

Thirty-six

$\mathcal{A}$ whisper in the dark.

"You're not going to teach him to be selfish, are you?"

Three twenty-two in the morning, glowed the clock. How can Leslie tell I'm awake? How can a deer tell when a leaf falls silent in her forest? She hears it breathing differently.

"I'm not teaching him to be anything," I whispered back. "I'm telling him what I think is true and he's going to have to decide for himself what he wants to believe."

"Why are you whispering?" she said.

"I don't want to wake you up."

"You already did," she whispered. "You changed to wake-breathing a minute ago. You're thinking about Dickie."

"Leslie," I said, testing her. "What am I doing now?"

She listened in the silence. "You're blinking your eyes."

"THERE IS NO POSSIBLE WAY FOR ANYBODY TO TELL THAT ANYBODY ELSE IS BLINKING THEIR EYES IN THE DARK!"

Silence. Then a whisper. "Do you want me to apologize because I have good hearing?"

I sighed.

A smaller whisper, defiant: "Well, I won't."

"What am I doing now?" I said.

"I don't know."

"I'm smiling."

She turned to face me, and I put my arm around her in the night. "What are you thinking about," she said, "that woke you up?"

"You'll make fun of me."

"I won't. Honest."

"I was thinking about good and evil."

"Oh, Richie! At three o'clock in the middle of the night you wake up thinking about good and evil?"

"Are you making fun of me?" I asked.

She softened. "It's just a question."

"Yes."

"What were you thinking?" she said.

"That for the first time I get it . . . there's no such thing."

"No such thing as good and evil?"

"No."

"What is there?"

"There's happy and unhappy," I said.

"Happy is good and unhappy is evil?"

"Completely subjective. It's all of it in our head!"

"Then what's happy and unhappy?"

"What is it for you?" I said.

"Happy is joy! Intense delight! Unhappy is depression, hopelessness, despair."

I should have known. I had assumed her words would be mine: happiness is a sense of well-being, unhappiness is the lack of it. But my wife has ever been the more intense of us two. I told her my definition.

"Isn't that a little bland?" she said. " 'A sense of well-being'?"

"I need a definition that doesn't have a fifty-foot drop between the bottom of happy and the top of unhappy. What do you call that in-between place?"

"I call it okay."

"I don't have an okay," I said. "I have a sense of well-being."

"Okay," she said. "Now what?"

"Help me find any situation in which Good is not defined by the heart as 'Makes me happy.' Or one in which Bad is not 'Makes me unhappy.' "

"Love is good," she said.

"Love makes me happy," I answered.

"Terrorism is evil."

"You can do better than that, sweetie. Terrorism makes me unhappy."

"It's good when we make love together," she said, pressing her warm body against me in the dark.

"It makes us happy," I said, clinging desperately to intellect.

She pulled away. "Oh, Richie, what are you getting at?"

"No matter how I look at it, it keeps coming out that morality is up to us!"

"Of course it's up to us," she said. "That's what woke you up?"

"Don't you see, Wookie? Good and evil are not what our parents told us, not what our church tells us, or our country, not what anybody else tells us! All of us decide good and evil for ourselves, automatically, by choosing what we want to do!"

"Uh-oh," she said. "Please never write a word of this."

"I'm only thinking. And it feels strange because I can't find any way around it!"

"Please . . ."

"Try this," I said, "from the book of Genesis, about creation: *And God saw that it was good.*"

"You're going to tell me this means God was happy."

"Of course!"

"You don't believe in a God who even sees the world," she said, "or who has any more emotion than arithmetic. How can your God be happy?"

"The writer of Genesis, the silly goose, didn't check with me before he took out his pencil. In his book, God's full of feelings—glad and sad, furious and scheming and vengeful. Good and evil weren't absolute, they were measures of God's happiness. He was writing a story, and that's what he had in mind: *If I think God would be happy about this, I'll call it 'good.'*" I fretted at the hour. "I need examples where people use 'good' and 'evil,' but it's dark and I can't look any up."

"Good."

"That makes you happy?" I said.

"Of course. Otherwise you'll be up turning on lights, getting books, the computer, chattering away, and we'll be up all night."

"So it makes you happy that it's dark and you're probably not going to be disturbed with me carrying on about good and evil all night. Naturally you say 'Good.' "

"Just don't write it," she said. "You'll have every extremist . . . no, you'll have every *reasonable* human being in the country up late, stuffing your books through shredders!"

"Leslie, this is nothing more than a curiosity. That we discover morals are personal does not mean they're suddenly the opposite of what they were; we don't turn into a homicidal maniac the second we realize we can be one if we want to. We're thoughtful, kind, courteous, loving to each other, we risk our lives to save somebody in distress because we *like to be that way,* not because we think God will be mad at us or Dad would disapprove if we didn't. *We're* responsible for our character, not Dad, not God . . ."

She was unmoved. "Please, no. If you write good is what makes us happy, can't you see the rationalizing? 'Richard Bach says good is what makes me happy. I love stealing trains, so stealing trains is good and how can anybody prosecute me for doing good by trotting home with the company locomotive in my lunchbox? Anyhow, it was Richard Bach's idea.' And there you'll be, on trial along with every happy train-thief . . ."

"Then I'll have to testify in court," I said. " 'The wise,

Your Honor, consider consequence before rushing to act. It may be our heart's delight and therefore good for the moment to go nipping off with somebody else's diesel turbine, but unless the range of consequences is also our heart's delight, we'd be happier rethinking the caper.' "

She sighed, impatient questions unspoken.

"Begging Your Honor's indulgence," I said. "Every action has its probable, its possible, and its unexpected consequences. Good—when all of these consequences are in the interest of the thoughtful person's long-term sense of well-being—will result from each following consequence as well as from the original act. 'I probably won't get caught' is not the same as 'I'll have a sense of well-being for the rest of my life from doing what I'm going to do right now.'

"Your Honor, I submit that since our prisoner is unhappy to stand in this courtroom, *he was not in fact acting in his own best interests* when he slipped that locomotive into his lunchbox, and he stands, by definition, convicted of unwisdom, his theft revealed as a bad idea!"

"Inventive," said Leslie. "But have you considered that good takes its meaning from general agreement, that good is what most people over the centuries have found to be positive and life-affirming? And have you considered that it might not be in your best interest, and therefore Bad, to spend the rest of your life delivering such arguments in court? And shall we leave it at that and go to sleep?"

"If most people think it's good to kill spiders," I said, "are we bad to set them free? Are we expected to run our lives by what other people think?"

"You know what I mean."

"Read the dictionary," I said. "Every word that judges value is circular. *Good* is *right* is *moral* is *proper* is *just* is *good*. But check the examples and they're not circular at all: Every one says *makes me happy*! I'll get the dictionary!"

"Please, no," she begged.

"What did you do about the war in Vietnam, Wookie? The President thought it was a good war and so did most people. So did I, until I met you. It made most of us happy, thinking we were defending an innocent country from a wicked aggressor. But not you! What you learned about it *did not make you happy*—you started the speaker's bureau against it, and the concerts, and the marches . . ."

"Richie?"

"Yes?"

"You may be right about good and evil. Let's talk about it tomorrow."

"Every time we say *Great!* we mean our sense of well-being has increased, every time we say *Damn!* or *Oh, no!*

we mean it's decreased. Every hour we're checking good and bad, right and wrong. We can listen to ourselves minute by minute and track our own ethics!"

"Sleep is good," she said. "Sleep would make me happy."

"If I lie here without a peep and go through every example I can think, switching *makes me happy* for good and right and wonderful and great and fine and terrific and *makes me unhappy* for evil and bad and wrong and terrible and sinful and wicked, will that keep you awake?"

She curled against my side, buried her head in her pillow. "No. As long as you don't blink."

In the dark, quietly, I smiled.

Thirty-seven

No sooner had I drifted asleep, head full of goods and evils . . .

✦

"I can't believe what you're thinking! Good is what makes you happy?"

"Believe it or not, Dickie," I said. "Thinking is not a crime."

"And if it were, you'd probably do it anyway."

The hilltop was greener than ever, and now down the slope bloomed rivers of tiny flowers, mostly yellows and blues that Leslie could have named on sight.

"How do you know what I'm thinking?" I said. "Did I

give you the key to my mind? Are you watching everything I do?"

Instead of a stone, wordless, he handed me a balsa model glider of twelve-inch wingspan, a lump of clay on its nose for balance.

"I don't watch anything," he said. "I don't see your life unless you let me. But lately I know what you're learning. That hasn't happened before."

Was it an invasion of privacy, to find him closer in my mind? Did it make me uncomfortable, that he was coming to know what I knew as I learned it?

I smiled. "Well, you're growing up."

He looked at me surprised. "I'm not. Don't you remember? I'm nine, Richard, and I always will be."

"Then why do you want to know all that I know, if not to try like you said a life with all my advantages and not my mistakes?"

"I didn't say I'd live it myself, I said I want to know what it would be like, to live it. To the man I'll become who acts on what I learn from you, I'll still be nine, same as I am for you. Tell me what's true . . . I don't know what to think about good and evil, and I need to know!"

"What isn't clear?" I said. "Good is what makes you . . ."

"It's too . . . simplistic!" he said, relishing the word. "*I* could come up with that!"

"Oh, come on, Captain. First you're not dumb, second the simplest things are most often the truest, third it's me, fifty years out, the guy with the learning you're looking for. Is it simplistic, when you hear *'Good!'* and before you agree, to consider who's saying they're happy and why?"

I balanced the glider, pushed it forward on the air. It took a mind of its own, dived straight into the ground from four feet up. A little nose-heavy, I could tell.

"There's got to be more to good," he said, "than does it make me happy."

"Sure there's more to it. Short-term gratification may not be long-term happy and we have to think, to tell the difference. In every they-sold-their-soul-to-the-devil story, the deal with Satan is the same: I'll trade long-term happiness for short-term pleasure, and the moral is always: *not too smart a deal!*

"Then there's a consensus good and evil, soft-edged values that match in a lot of people. Cultures may not agree between them on what's good and what isn't, but each of them, within itself, generally does."

"Does it have to be so hazy? Why can't it be clear? I have clear definitions."

"Murder is . . ."

"Bad," he said, no hesitating.

"Charity is . . ."

"Good."

I trimmed some clay from the nose of the little glider. "To be a conscientious objector in wartime is . . ."

"Hm."

"Is it good or bad," I asked again, "to be a conscientious objector in wartime?"

"What's the war? Are we defending ourselves or are we attacking some helpless little country?"

"There," I said. "As soon as you find one situation where good and evil depend on circumstance, the whole concept goes subjective, and it's never again the clear choice that we thought it was. Like any other value judgment, we have to say this is good *for me*, that's bad *for me*."

I launched the little glider again, carefully. It climbed abruptly, stalled, crashed gently into the grass.

"One exception doesn't change the rule!"

"No," I said, retrieving the glider and frowning over its weight-and-balance problem, adding a little clay back to the nose, "but one exception shows a million others."

"Show me."

"Is murder evil when it's self-defense? Is murder wrong when we kill enemies in wartime? Is murder immoral when a doctor grants the thoughtful deliberate wish of her patient in terminal illness and unbearable pain?"

"According to you, it's not possible to kill," he said. "Life Is, and we can't create it or destroy it."

"Life, Dickie, Is. It doesn't have rules. But you and I, we're talking games, now, spacetime, assumptions about appearances, institutionalized good and cultural evil, societies where real is what seems to be and Principle goes unnoticed."

"There's no real right or wrong?"

"There's no absolute Right and Wrong. The only absolute is Life Is."

"So I can do anything I want and there will be no consequences? I'm free to go out there and cheat and steal and kill and there's no consequence if my own personal morality says that's okay?"

"Of course you're free to do it," I said. "But there are consequences, which you may decide are not okay."

"Such as?"

"Such as your deed wears at your mind for the rest of your life. Or you languish in prison for seven to twelve years. Or you die surprised: you thought your victim was helpless and she turned out to be armed. In the world of appearances there are infinite consequences, infinite balances for any choice you make."

"For every choice," he said, "no matter what?"

"No matter what."

He squashed his thumb-tip with his finger. "For every single teeny-tiny this-big choice?"

"Try it," I said. "What choice has no consequences?"

I launched the little plane for the third time. It dove for the ground, leveled above the grasstops and skimmed thirty feet before it landed, gentle as a moth. Not bad, for three tries flying.

"Are there consequences for being a writer?"

"Yes," I said. "Every day I can sleep till noon."

"Oh, come on . . ."

I walked to pick the glider from the grass. "Dickie, don't you understand? There's always some . . . aftermath, good and bad . . ."

". . . makes-me-happy or makes-me-unhappy . . ." he explained for us both.

". . . for doing anything we choose to do," I finished, "for being anyone we decide to be."

"What about writing is a bad consequence?" he said.

Walking back, I couldn't decipher his look, couldn't tell why he asked.

"I wrote a book about diet, years ago, and said that for some of us, losing ten pounds might be a good idea."

"That's a bad consequence of being a writer?"

"No," I told him. "The consequence that made me unhappy was that one of my readers agreed, quoted me as his authority, and cut off his head to lose the weight."

Eyes like dinner-plates. "WHAT?"

303

"He didn't understand what I wrote, Dickie, but he did lose the ten pounds."

"You're kidding!"

"Not by much," I said. "I wrote a book, years ago, about someone who was not frightened of dying. A young man read the book, decided that he wasn't afraid of dying, either, and he killed himself."

"You're still kidding."

"No. True story." I sat in the grass, holding the airplane.

"Why did he do it?"

"He was in love, his girlfriend's parents didn't approve of him, said they'd send their daughter away so the two would never see each other again. The lovers decided to kill themselves, drove high-speed into a wall. She survived the crash, he didn't."

"Why didn't they just run away together?"

"Good question."

"If I were willing to die over something, Richard, I'd sure be willing to do anything less! And less-than-dying includes some pretty drastic acts."

"Such as?" What did I think was drastic when I was nine?

"Pack my scout-knife and matches and take some food and hike away into the mountains with her."

I remembered my old last-ditch escape; off into the steep wilderness that loomed every day on the horizon, past the edge of my hometown. I waited for more.

"If I knew how to drive, I'd drive to Montana with her. Or we'd stow away together on a freighter to New Zealand."

Sure enough, escape was his first thought. If it were time for drastic today, I thought, I'd still choose escape.

"I'd talk with her parents," he went on, "promise to cut their lawn for the rest of their lives, show them my great report cards and get fifty of my friends to come in and tell them I'm a really nice guy."

I nodded.

"Holy cow, her mom and dad didn't *own* her, did they?"

"Not forever," I said. "Not for a second, to tell my truth, but my truth probably wasn't theirs."

305

"Let her move," he said. "I'd write her letters in care of the first new friend wherever she went, keep writing until I was old enough to go get her."

"Could do."

"I'd work and send her money to call me whenever she wanted. We'd plan on the phone, and find each other again."

I waited.

"Patience. Sooner or later we'd both be on our own, no parents, and nobody could stop us from being together."

In five minutes the boy had five plans short of suicide to face the test the girl's parents had built, a plan a minute. In a day, I thought, couldn't my young reader have done the same?

If the poor kid had been dangling by a string over a lake of alligators and the string chafed through, I'd allow that his choices were limited, but even then dying is nowhere near inevitable. I used to swim with alligators in Florida; they're not all man-eaters. Even when they are, if they're not hungry or if they're meditating while you float by, it's like any other dip in the lake.

I tossed the little airplane. It climbed, leveled, soared out over the edge of the hill, out of sight.

Dying's a once-in-a-lifetime statement, I thought, wishing my reckless reader here with Dickie and me. Killing ourselves at sixteen doesn't qualify as winning the game we came here to play.

And get this straight, I thought to him: if you're going to use my book to justify suicide, you need my written permission, certified mail, before you do it. Skip that and I'll be miffed as hell, any reader of mine forgot spacetime's our sport, bowed so low to a world of mirrors.

I was quiet for a while, thinking about his choice.

"How would it feel, Dickie? You kill yourself in your crash, you lift out of the body all smashed there at the wheel, and then you realize, *Oh, no! We could have eloped to Auckland! Have I been a silly goose or what?*"

"Too late," he said. "According to you, I'd have to get in line again, get myself born as a baby a whole lot more helpless than any teenager, I'd have to start over: learn how to talk, learn how to walk, learn how to count, go to kindergarten, do what grown-ups say because I'm little and they're big . . ."

We don't have to get in line again, I thought. We don't have to do anything. We *want* to do it again, try to get it right, mend a thoughtless act.

For the first time since we met, the boy I was felt sorry

for the man I am. "What were the consequences," he said quietly, "for writing a book that somebody didn't understand?"

"I felt this huge tension, Dickie, I still do. I want to talk to him, I want to hear him tell me his other choices."

"You can't. He's dead."

Who knows, I thought. Maybe by the time the next book is done, she'll be able to read.

Thirty-eight

*D*ickie left me alone for a while, walked away without good-bye.

Whenever something terrible happens to us, or when we can't see our way out, it's nice to hear somebody say, "It's okay," even when it's our own voice speaking.

It's okay is a cosmic truth, I thought, and felt the tension drain away. My unmet suicide has his lessons to learn, so do we all. It's okay. If there were nothing here for us to learn, we wouldn't bother to pay the fare.

I looked past the hillside to the mountains, air clear as diamond across the miles between. Flying, there's no distance. Any place on earth, we can go: distant village, mountains snowy and aloof, coral island, swirling cloud-top. Stormy days, we can climb up and visit the sun, if we want. Trust our instruments, do not stop climbing no matter fog or rain or wind, and before long we will break out on top. Cosmic law, given to flyers to prove in daily life.

Time to wake up, I thought, time to shift to a different dream.

As I set about to make the shift, I saw the top of Dickie's head appear over the hillside and he came trudging back, the little glider in his hand.

"It really flew, Richard! It was way, way down the hill! You really can fly airplanes! How do you do that?"

"Practice," I said, covering luck with modesty.

"Is the name a secret?" he asked, knowing I didn't know what name, wanting me to ask.

"What name?"

"The name of your religion."

"It doesn't have a name, Dickie, it never will, and it's not a religion. An organized religion, anyway. Organized religion is God-in-a-web, the Great Spider at the center of a thousand doctrines and rituals and mandatory believings. People die in that web. Please, no organization!"

He smiled at me. "You have a nameless disorganized

religion? You have a something, that you believe. You have a . . . what?"

"I have a way of finding what is true for me, and it's not finished yet. It's . . . it's an experimental personal philosophy, and it will never have a name. You know why." I knew he didn't know why, but he deserved the courtesy, I thought, of being allowed to guess.

"Because a name is a label," he said, "and as soon as there's a label the ideas disappear and out comes label-worship and label-bashing and instead of living by a theme of ideas people begin dying for labels, and the last thing you think the world needs is a new religion?"

I stared at him. "Good guess."

"Does it have a symbol, your nameless experimental personal private philosophy?"

"Of course not. A symbol is just as bad . . ."

"I understand," he said. "But wouldn't it be different, just for you, just for fun, to have a symbol to represent your way of thinking, to remind you it has no name and it never will? And safe, too. Something that can't be put into words won't likely become a label."

"Cute idea," I said. "What matters, though, is how I use

what I know, every minute of every day; how I use it to remember, in the midst of the game."

He held on to his question. "If there were a symbol, in your mind, what would it be?" he asked. "Not a star, not a crescent, not a cross, probably."

I laughed. "No, Dickie, not a cross. A cross without the bar. I don't like bars."

"A cross without the bar," he said, "is the number one."

"You've got it," I said. "One in binary arithmetic means Not-Nothing, Is instead of Isn't. One is the number of Life, no matter how many dreams."

"A cross without the bar is a capital *I*."

"To remind me this nameless path is my own personal way of thinking, not to be suggested to anyone unless they ask and then only if that day I feel like saying, which for anyone but you I do not."

"A cross without the bar is a little *l*."

"To remind me there's the test, the question waiting at the end of every dream: *How well, this time, did you express love?*"

"That's it," he said. "*I*. The perfect symbol."

"No symbols, not a chance," I said. "Not on your life."

"Of course not on my life," he said. "There's only one life."

He held the glider and sat in the grass a few inches from my knee. "I have to decide, Richard, before much longer," he said.

"Decide what?"

He looked at me surprised, as though I should have known, and then accepting . . . there's no reason I should.

"Decide to go," he said. "I guess I need some advice."

His voice was a flickered memory of my brother's, and it frightened me a little.

Dickie's an aspect of life just as real and just as unreal as any Richard Bach, I thought, he can no more die than I can. And besides, I like him, we've come to trust each other, we're friends now, and there's too much left to say. What's this talk about going?

"I don't know if it happens to everyone or not," he said. "But with you and me, there's a time I have to decide whether to be here for you or to fade out again. Me and the rest of your childhood."

313

"Have I learned so little," I asked, "that you can pick it all up so fast, and be gone?"

"Are there no consequences," he answered, "for leaving me locked away fifty years?"

As if he had thrown a rock at my head. I blinked in the shock of it, before I saw that he didn't mean revenge. He was simply asking the question, considering options.

"You're right," he said. "I haven't learned it all. But I've pretty well listened to what you think is true." He handed me the little glider. "Thank you, Richard."

Dickie is not my brother, I thought. How can I feel the way I did when Bobby died? "You never said anything about decisions, or leaving," I said. "You're an imaginary child, an imaginary me, you're nobody real. You can't leave me!"

"You're an imaginary grown-up," he said, "you tell me you're one of my futures. I trust you, I believe you, I think you're probably right. But if you're going to change now and tell me that anybody who doesn't have a body, yourself included at the moment, isn't real then I haven't under-stood a word you've said. You want to start over and teach me that real is what I see with my eyes? I pretty much doubt that, Richard, and I'm no grown-up."

Sympathize with anything, know its feelings in our own

314

heart, and we're joined by love: to a doll, to a pet, to a child we've met in our mind. Once that happens, what can break love's weld?

"I'm sorry," I said. "That was dumb for me to say. If it's time for you to go, it's time. I'm acting like a kid."

He looked at me curiously when I said that, cocked his head to be sure I wasn't making fun.

"Knowing what you know," he said, "I can start a lifetime so different from yours you'll never guess it was me launched it when we meet again face-to-face. That'll be fun."

"Yep," I said. A long silence. "Time for you to be on your way, I guess."

"For your sake, too," he said. "Most of your life you've been trying to drop your childhood, it's been dead weight. I haven't let you do it. I wouldn't die, in my cell, and I wouldn't let you go. But you opened the door. A little late, but you opened the door. Thanks for the rain in my desert."

"Don't go," I said. "We're friends."

"Richard, you're nearly sixty! Don't you want to keep on learning? Don't you want to cut away the excess baggage? Your childhood is cargo I know how to drop!"

"I'm what?" I said. "I'm nearly what?"

"You're nearly sixty. I'm nine and you're fifty years in my future. You're nearly sixty." Was that grin his declaration of independence?

"I don't believe in nine, you know that. I don't believe in sixty. We are not creatures built from time . . ."

He watched me in tolerance, as though I were the child.

"Dickie," I said. "Pickle-ball, chess, foils or épées or sabers, track or field or pool or range. Pick your test, pick your age. Take nineteen. Twenty-eight? Forty. I will take you on at any belief of any age you pick, and I swear . . . I'll thrash you flat! *Nearly sixty what is that supposed to mean?*"

He watched me for a moment, the grin lingering, the boy more friend than child. Then something happened behind his eyes, as though a clock had chimed and his time was up. He thanked me with a nod, recovered his decision.

"Sixty," he said, "is too long for you to carry a childhood you barely remember. Let me do one thing for you. Let me lift that load. And we'll let each other go."

Thirty-nine

*L*eslie put down her book: *Amiable Ways to Suggest Alternate Homesites for Organic Garden Pests*. "What's on your mind, sweetie?" she said. "What's worrying you?"

I lay next to her in bed, staring at the ceiling. "Nothing. Just thinking."

"Oh," she said. "Okay." She went back to reading.

I had decided not to mention Dickie's decision until I had thought it through, until I had spent another hour or ten reviewing the odd friendship, why it had mattered so much to me, what other futures could have happened had he chosen not to go.

As he had promised, I felt lighter without the old childhood dogging me. The doubt of decades was gone, the uneasy suspicion that I had forgotten something desperately important from my past life as a child. With his help I had climbed beyond that time, and the hazy distant view of yesterday was finally out of sight.

"A quick study," said Leslie, still reading her book.

"Who?"

"Dickie," she said. "He learned everything he wanted from you and he's gone?"

"What makes you say that?"

"Just guessing," she said. "But I'd have to be a rock, not to pick up your Distress-from-Incompletion waves."

It will be nice, someday, to have an adventure all thought-through and settled, then pick my time and tell my wife beginning, middle, end and meaning. That will happen, I thought, around the time that hell freezes solid.

"Well, yes."

"Did he come to give you something, or to get something from you?" She said it as if she had the answer already picked.

"He wanted to learn," I said, "and it was fun to show him. Now he knows just about everything I know and it's up to him to decide what to do with it. I'm not part of any future of his but this one."

"You mean no more to him than that," she said, question turned quiet statement. "Do you miss him?"

"I don't think I could fairly say that," I said. "I'll remember him. I'll think about him."

She smiled at my ways. "Did you have a hard time teaching him to rationalize away every shred of human feeling, or was he a quick study on that, too?"

"Oh, Wookie, don't be silly! I'm a rational soul, I won't soon be changing my spots, you'd be lost if I did. We balance perfectly, you and me, on our little see-saw, and you don't want me jumping all my weight to your side tell me if I'm wrong."

"Rational or feeling," she said, "it doesn't matter. I've decided to keep you."

"Thank you, sweet." I moved closer, turned out my light, slid my arm beneath her pillow, closed my eyes to sleep. "It would be so cold, without you."

"You're learning, aren't you?" she said.

"No, sweet," I murmured. "For once in my life I was the teacher, not the student."

"M-hm."

She returned to her book and read till I was nearly gone.

"Next time you see him," she said, "tell Dickie I love him too."

Forty

*T*hat night, three A.M., I slammed awake in the dark, eyes wide staring into black, a double-take months over-due: Dickie remembers the childhood I've forgotten! He remembers *from the first minute!*

Two ends of a lifetime, we had been, reaching toward a center that neither of us could find alone. In the hours we spent together, I thought, all I had to do was ask! He still kept a single adventure, the key to all that I had come to believe, the scene I needed to touch one time, grown up.

He can't be gone!

I squeezed my eyes shut, forced myself to relax, brought his face back to mind, clear and bright, melted into it.

A moment later I stood on a hillside where forest met meadow, a spiral galaxy of tiny silver flowers shining around me. Away below on one hand lay an ocean nearly as dark as the sky, a diamond river shimmering toward it. On the other, as far as I could see, stretched a broad plain to horizons of pristine hills and valleys. Deserted and still, Eden revisited.

Changed from the hilltop I knew, yet impossibly familiar. Where had I seen this place before? He had to be near.

I found him perched on a rock ledge, the same boy unchanged, launching a glider. As if he slid it into the sky with a tiny pilot aboard, it slanted over the green, found the lift band at the edge of the slope, banked hard into the rising air and climbed.

A startling sight. How did he make that happen? I didn't wait to watch.

"You remember my childhood!" I said, no hello. "All of it! Don't you?"

"Of course I do," he said. "Just because you shut it out doesn't mean it's lost."

"You remember being born!"

All along, I thought, he's had the answer. Dickie knows what changes our serene spirit from living light into an I-never-asked-for-this infant screaming in the dark. The link I never found and couldn't imagine.

"I need that memory," I said.

A flash of mock surprise. "I thought you'd never ask."

He fished in his shirt pocket and brought forth a little dome of crystal turned faintest amber, no larger than a lemondrop.

"Built to last forever," he said. "Nothing can open it but your wish to know." He held it out to me. "Careful, it'll break when you touch. You're sure you want this?"

I took it from his hand. Lighter than eggshell, the little thing. Why not, this gentle peace-filled glide of my first day on earth, its mystery wrapped in rose petal. So delicate!

No sooner had I brushed the dainty surface with my fingertip than it shattered in my hand, the hour before my birth day.

Forty-one

At the time, I remembered, it was a great idea.

Adventure! Romance! Joined again with old friends, hurling myself into one last battle with my handpicked circle of grand bright-flame enemies. This time they'll be pussycats! Worst possible outcome: a scratch or two should I forget who I am for a minute, should I blink at their Seems to Be.

Most unlikely, that scratch. I remember! Nevermore the old disasters when I lost that knowing, fought lifetimes against phantoms, got myself hammered to dust, wondered my last moment why I'd ever been born.

Never again. Powers I've learned, no enemy can match. Life in spacetime, it's Snap City, hey? I am so smart at this game, I am so utterly invulnerable to any weapon, so totally secure in knowing, that I shall glide laughing through that ring of dragons that powdered me so many times before. Rested, restored, armed with unshakable understanding of reality instead of my old belief in fictions, what in earth can scratch me now?

Unafraid is not the word . . . this is going to be FUN!

One last lifetime, one final match in the game, to prove victory never has to be hard, to show I've learned forever the easy knowing grace from which every real triumph is built.

Remember who you are, cowboy, never believe what you see around you, and this is gonna be a *Piece! Of! Cake!*

Armed thus, heedless of dragons, I stepped off the edge, and everything went black.

✦

How strange it felt, being born!

Hours ago I was safe, floating happy, systems working warm and well, now the mind's a control room at nuclear meltdown, full emergency. A hundred terror-bright death-red warnings flashing: breathe now or die; eat now or die; falls kill; fire kills; water kills; enemies in the dark; dog looks tame, eats babies.

Never seen so many bright cautions screaming and now I'm wide open VUL-NER-A-BL, spelled *p o w e r l e s s* and I can't even sob the word for "Help!"

One person near. Mom, I hate to be self-centered but I'd just as soon you stay close till I'm checked out on dangers, till I'm armed and armored, till I'm about thirty, please, and by the way tell me what am I doing here? I seem to have forgotten . . . did I pick this life for me or did you and would you care to tell me for what possible crazy reason why?

She had answers but my questions came out cries, and there-there little one is not much help when I know the wind chill is thirty below outside and I start shivering at sixty-eight above. The only choice was to close eyes, shut down systems, sleep.

And sleeping drift back to smooth soft emerald-amber hillsides, jump and I don't fall but float, a flare of dandelion light airborne. Sleeping come home again, come smart again in language without words, teachers and students everyone to each other, purpose and sense to everything.

YOU WOULD NOT BELIEVE! I told them. Next time I say this sounds like fun, another life in spacetime, will you catch me with a net? Didn't you see I was CRAZY? They hit you with all their limits at once, the second you touch down on earth . . . space-limits time-limits: I'm separate and different from everybody else, trapped in the Jell-O mold of a little TINY creature, a clumsy miniature headlong straitjacket body dwarfed by every other known object can't mindlink can't homecome can't even fly and the gravity's enormous, I'm heavier than elephants in tar, I'm frailer than lace-wing butterflies, everything everywhere ice and steel except Mom and a blanket, boundaries like daggers at my throat, rules I can't guess, curtain's up on a play I have to write my own part in words I don't know with a mind that's mostly hash trying to work a mouth that can't even say let me out of here.

Spacetime's mad enough in theory . . . in practice it's madness twisted, a minute for grown-ups is days for me, clunk-clunk-clunk: universes splitting away every second and nobody notices, noses to the grindstone of a million choices turned to only one, all put to bed in a changeless past by a future that's everybody's guess.

This is play, isn't it? Unreal I was warned, but this is unreal with a vengeance, this is impossible challenge: transform this three-strikes-against-me infant bodymind into somebody who will at best barely begin to reflect who I am and at worst turn twig-in-the-rapids never made it to dry land swept hopeless over the falls muttering what's it all about, who can *remember* in all that noise?

I was crazy to choose it, but I might as well give it a go, worst thing that can happen is with luck the dog will eat me and I'll be out of this trapdoor universe and home again.

Waking, I didn't even remember that.

✦

I was observer, just removed from ghosthood—those I watched could watch me back. Cute little guy, they told my mother, deep-soul grateful they'd never be my age again. He's so lucky! Look at those wide eyes . . . innocent, happy, safe.

Wrong. Wrong. Wrong.

I was fighting the biggest battles of my lifetime, those first hours, and losing them, row on row of falling dominoes.

"I am," I told the world. "I am neverborn, neverdying individual expression of infinite life, choosing spacetime for my schoolyard and playground. Came here for the fun of it, to join again with old friends, to challenge again grand dear enemies . . ."

Like being kicked in the face with an iron boot, such were my enemies. They didn't use words, didn't need 'em.

Pain! Welcome to spacetime, Land of No Other Choice. What you see is what there is, fella. It's just blurs now, but the better you see, the worse it gets. Here is frost, here is hunger, here is thirst, here is your body which is all there is of you. No sweeping infinite life now. All that stands between you and sudden death are two mere mortals you have barely met, two not all so sure they want to be your parents.

"I remember life before I came! I didn't need to breathe or eat, then, I didn't need a body to live and I lived! I chose my parents, and they chose me! I chose this time! I remember . . ."

You remember dreams! Glimmers in your empty infant brain. Show us that life, point it out for us. Can't do it? Try hard! Forgotten where it is? So soon?

Try this, infant . . . hold your breath for three minutes, step through the ice for five, sleep in the snow for ten, leave your mother for a day. Try this, then come tell us about Infinite Life!

Foggy newborn mind aswirl, losing a battle a minute. No time to think, physical world owns time. The world's fighting on its own ground, nothing's true but what it sees with its eyes and touches with its fingers. No proof accepted but physical proof, everything else is scorn-food.

I'm tripped off-balance, back to the wall. Infants don't know which end of a sword to hold. I'm outnumbered and I'm getting cut to shreds by the dullest of that wicked army, child's play, cut that little rebel before he learns to see.

This world is flint and stone, it hurts too much. I'm ribbons and blood hanging on, and Mom doesn't even know I'm fighting for my life.

329

"It's okay, little one, don't you cry. Everything's okay . . ."

Mom! I cried wordless. Help me!

Not all talk is words, and sometimes mothers tell more than they know when children cry.

She stroked my head. "Little one. The dragons outnumber you, and they lie. You *can* choose. Two choices. One: Call their bluff, don't listen to their limits, my baby. Close your eyes, lift your spirit, remember who you are, beyond space, beyond time, never born, never dying . . ."

I relaxed, let go.

". . . and the physical world will raise a fist in victory —Lo! Dead! All eyes to swear your tiny body unbreathing, all fingers agree no pulse, sign a scroll to call your victory death."

She held me to her face. "Another choice: Win by losing. Before your outer walls break, as break they must if you are to stay, build an inner place to protect your truth. Protect that you are infinite life, choosing its playground; protect that the world you know exists with your consent and for your own good reasons; protect that your purpose and mission is to shine love in your own playful way, in the moments you decide will be most dramatic. The dragons are your *friends*!"

I listened to my mother remembering, to her prism life-line linking me at once between the sunlight from which I came and this place of shifting dark glass and attacks before dawn.

She looked into my eyes becoming saucers gazing astonished into hers. "Truth held fast?" she asked, her whisper a secret between us. "Pour crystal, now, around the center of your being, deeper and stronger than space and time, pour a shield that nothing can break away . . ."

But Mother, I blinked, listening, losing. Even you are space and time. You are here and not there. You are with me now and one day you will die . . .

"That's right," she murmured. "Listen to your dragons. I am trapped in spacetime just as you are. I will die, and your brothers, and your father, too. And you will be alone. Let go. Surrender. Let your walls go, let them tumble away, stones become sand. Let the world flood itself through you, over you, learn its lies, swim in them, don't resist. And way inside, remember what you've locked safe away, and one day twenty years from now, little one, sixty years from now, touch your truth, and laugh . . ."

I trusted her and I let go, surrendered to dragons days after I was born, watched my walls burst to froth before blue-mountain tidal waves: no choice, no questions, life is miserable short unfair there's no purpose we are no fledglings poised to soar we are lemmings hurled brainless over cliffs of chance, for no reason at all. Welcome to earth, stupid.

"Hey, wow!" I said. "Great to be here!"

✦

That's better, my dragons hissed, curling close about me. Life is so much easier when you do not resist. You have nothing to remember, everything to learn.

Your eyes are so closed to us—open your eyes, now.

Your body is so relaxed—tense your body, now.

Your mind is so wide—focus your mind, now.

Your soul is so safe—give up your soul, now.

They spoke in relays, never stopping.

You are in a deep, sound waking sleep. Every word we utter sends you deeper and deeper into noisy, restless waking. Do not wonder, do not question.

You have something on your mind. Speak it, and as you do, you will sink deeper and deeper . . .

"Thank you," I said. "So much to learn!"

Good. Yes. Mortals love to learn, and our gift to you is that you will always love to learn. Learn this:

Appearance is reality. What you see is what is real. What you touch is what is real. What you hear and taste and smell is real. What you think is not real, what you hope does not exist. Test Number One: What is reality?

"Appearance is reality," I said.

Good. Excellent student. Deep, sleep. So much to learn:

Reality changes with time.
Atoms form life, rule life, end life.
Destiny is chance.
Some people are lucky, some are not.
To live is to win, to gain, to become somebody; to die is to lose, to disappear, to become nobody.

Test Number Two, a little harder now: What changes reality?

"Time," I said. "And space."

Time is the answer. Why do you say space?

"Because reality is different in different places."

Good! "Time" is the answer, but space is true, too. Already you understand! You are thinking creatively. Do you understand creativity?

"Yes. Nothing exists until it is created physically, in space and time. Before it is created it is unreal. After it is destroyed it is unreal. Everything is created, everything is destroyed. It is all a matter of time."

What lies beyond space?

"Nothing."

What exists after time?

"Nothing."

Your mother will teach you to walk. Why will you always walk through doorways and never walk through walls?

"Walls are limits. Nobody walks through walls because walls are solid, and I cannot pass through solids without being destroyed. Mom and Dad do not walk through walls, and they are big and powerful. No one is more powerful than the limits of space and time, least of all me."

Good. Everything has limits. There are limits to resources. There are limits to food, air, water, shelter, ideas. The more you use, the less there is for others. Others are older and stronger and wiser than you, they were first, they have seniority. Therefore remember:

Children are not often to be seen, and if seen they are not to be heard. Children must never annoy grown-ups.

Children do not think, or if they do, their thinking is such a stumbling rudimentary failure that their mind is vacant gravel. A child cannot imagine anything new or different or significant.

Stay in your place. Always consider: What will people say? Don't upset anyone because you are so spiderweb frail that for the first years of your life even weaklings can kill you barehand.

Force is power.

Anger is the only warning you'll ever get.

Fear is no defense.

Test: What is the only world that ever was or ever will be?

"The world that I see with my eyes."

Where did you come from?

"I come from nowhere, I am going nowhere. There is no purpose."

Good! Origin is luck. Body is machine; it is carbon, hydrogen, oxygen, running on organic fuel. Body controls mind, mind is random electrical activity through brain.

There is one physical reality, it does not require your consent for its existence, and it goes on separate from your mind or your life. Your thought has zero effect on the reality of the physical world. There is no such thing as nonphysical reality.

Refuse these ideas and you will die. Questions?

"Teach me more."

The world had too many problems before you came and it does not need another. No one cares about who you are or what you think. Every important idea has already been thought, every important book has been written, every lovely painting painted, every discovery made, every song sung, film produced, conversation finished. Every important life has been lived. You do not matter and you never will.

Test: Who cares about you?

"I care about me!"

Wrong. Again: Who cares about you?

"No one cares about me, and it is selfish conceit to care about myself. There are billions alive on this planet, I arrived without an invitation, the others will let me stay if I am quiet and obedient and don't eat much. Most of all quiet."

Correct. Everyone is separate from everyone else. All knowledge travels in words and numbers. You know nothing until someone teaches you. Everyone older is smarter than you. Everyone bigger is more powerful.

Value comes in objective bad-worse-worst, good-better-best. There is Right and Wrong, there is Good and Evil. Good and Right deserve to live, Evil and Wrong deserve to die.

You do not live for yourself, you live to please others, to help others.

There are many nations and languages in the world. You were born in the best nation, its language the best language, its political system the best system, its army the best army. You obey the commands you are given by your country, from any level of its authority, to fight and die for your nation, to keep it Number One.

Good guys win, bad guys lose.

"But everybody dies, so even good people lose, in the end?"

If good people die, they go to heaven, and are happy.

"But heaven cannot be seen with the eyes, and nothing is real that is not seen. You said!"

Heaven is a lie, to hide that dying is losing. Believe the lie.

Justice is when a bad person dies, tragedy is when a good person dies, death is the end of life.

Everything does not have an answer. The universe is unknowable. Nothing important makes sense.

"How can that all be true?"

It is all true. It is reality.

"Of course."

✦

Not ten hours on the planet and I was disarmed, the key for which I had paid a thousand lifetimes was buried under that deep lead-mass safety of accepting what everybody knows—life is the accident that happens before we slip and die.

338

Way below conscious thought: What the world doesn't need is one more fool. Why am I so desperate to be Joe Bubblehead yet again, what possibly can I gain from endless seeing-is-believing hypnotism, from unlearning everything I know is true? I'm growing up like every other child on this planet, swallowing whole everything the world suggests, and before much longer it'll be too late to remember. Do I remember now? Why did I come here at all?

The battle is over. The baby sleeps.

Forty-two

"What you knew before you were born isn't lost." His voice was soft as a breeze on the hilltop.

"You only hide it till you're tested, till it's time to re-member. Sure enough, when you want, you'll find some odd funny beautiful way to find it again."

I sat near him on the ledge of rock, my chin on my knees, trying to read the change in him.

I watched Dickie's eyes, then, for nearly a minute, not saying a word, wondered how I had known so much when I was him. I was a bright kid, sure enough, but I had a lot to learn, I wasn't *that* bright.

And then I reached a snail's conclusion, at long long last.

4th & San Carlos
P.O. Box 4082
Carmel-by-the-Sea
California 93921
408-624-4862
800-634-1300 CA only
408-625-5443 Fax

Carmel
Fireplace
Inn

Dan Sturges
General Manager

returned my gaze unblinking,
slowly to the corner of his

im. "You knew it all along,
to remember everything I
for mine. All these months,
been a test."

denied.

nce, barely moving his head.

"Donald Shimoda?"

Once more, imperceptibly.

"Jonathan Seagull."

The tiny smile remained, the unmoving nod, the eyes locked wordless on mine.

A sudden terrifying thought, but I couldn't keep from asking. "Dickie, you're not Shepherd, too, wrote the book for me to sign, a good health plan is money in the bank?"

The smile broadened.

341

I clutched my hair, not knowing whether to laugh or cry. "Kid, for God's sake! Do you mind? That's cheating!"

He enjoyed the sight, the soul behind a mask of the child I'd been. "How can life cheat somebody's got power tools?" he said. "How can life give mid-terms to somebody's done with tests? The point is to *remember*!"

I should have known, I thought. When will I learn to expect what I can't imagine will happen?

"If you wanted to find what I think I know," I said, "did it ever occur to you that you might just ask?"

He scoffed me with his smile. "And fill out your hold-harmless in three copies, listen to you censor your knowing so we don't misunderstand and drive ninety miles an hour into a wall? We don't want your cautions, Richard, we want your truth! We don't . . ."

"WHY? I'm not a faster-than-thought seagull, I'm not the Savior of the world, I'm not a multidimensional alternate-future light-form knows all the answers to every question ever asked! Why do you care about me?"

"What's the mystery, Richard? You're not some castaway on a lost-island planet. You think you've had no luck meeting your other lifetimes, learning with them? *Us!* You are *us*!"

He paused, searching for words I could understand. "You chose us for your teachers? We chose you, too. You care about what you're learning? We care, too. You think we're in your life because you love us? Can't you understand? *We love you too!*"

I pressed my hands to the rock, holding on. Why should it be so hard to know, that the ones we love, love us back?

"You never left, did you?" I said at last. "You've changed your face, you've gone invisible sometimes, but you've been here all along. The worst times, too, divorce and bankruptcy and failure and death?"

"Especially the worst times."

How can I be so dense? Through the hardest days of my life has always stayed that quiet watching assurance: *There's a reason you chose what's happening around you. Hang on, Richard, live your way through it the best you know, and in a bit you'll find out why.* Who dares say such a thing, who dares remind us but our own inner teachers, unruffled by what seems to be?

After months of testing me with questions, Dickie had nothing left to ask. My exam finished in silence, a single last connection:

"Dickie," I said, "you're the one, aren't you? You're captain of my hidden spaceship, waiting to take me home."

The faintest of smiles. "Wrong," he whispered. "You're the captain."

end

Epilog

The crew we sign aboard our inner ship are our navigators and gunners and helmsmen and counselors, all right, and they'll stay our friends for life. We meet them the moment we're ready or needful or curious to touch, the moment we dare imagine their being and call out for their help.

I doubt that's the last I'll see of Jonathan Seagull or Donald Shimoda or Pye or Shepherd, though I haven't a clue what they're stirring into the next exam, half a minute or a hundred centuries from now, and I'm not going to ask.

I know for sure it's not the last I'll see of Dickie. He's looking out through my eyes this moment, watching his past and his future blink into words on a laptop computer screen.

The little guy who needed to know everything I've

learned has found a home. The prisoner I had locked away lives now in a place with a view, high in my spirit, a fountain of questions splashing:

Richard, who do you think you are?

Who will you be next?

Which values are you choosing for stars to steer by, and which ones are you letting go?

What are you doing here, Captain, what would you rather be doing and why aren't you doing it now?

Show me how you learn about love.

We wait all these years to find someone who understands us, I thought, someone who accepts us as we are, someone with a wizard's power to melt stone to sunlight, who can bring us happiness in spite of trials, who can face our dragons in the night, who can transform us into the soul we choose to be. Just yesterday I found that magical Someone is the face we see in the mirror: It's us and our homemade masks.

All these years, and at last we meet.

Imagine that.